LEONA

DCOHE

NTHEM

USICAN

DTHEM

YSTIQUE

Cover designed by Fresh Lemon, insides designed by Hilite Design & Reprographics
Picture research by Jacqui Black

ISBN: 9781780383026
Order No: OP54406

Exclusive Distributors
Music Sales Limited,
14-15 Berners Street,
London, W1T 3LJ.

Music Sales Corporation,
257 Park Avenue South,
New York, NY 10010, USA.

Macmillan Distribution Services,
56 Parkwest Drive
Derrimut, Vic 3030,
Australia.

Every effort has been made to trace the copyright
holders of the photographs in this book but one or two
were unreachable. We would be grateful if the
photographers concerned would contact us.

Images by LFI, Getty, Rex Features and Alberto Manzano.

Printed in the EU

A catalogue record for this book Is available from the
British Library.

Visit Omnibus Press on the web at
www.omnibuspress.com

LEONARD COHEN
THE MUSIC AND THE MYSTIQUE

BY MAURICE RATCLIFF

OMNIBUS PRESS

LONDON / NEW YORK / PARIS / SYDNEY / COPENHAGEN / BERLIN / MADRID / TOKYO

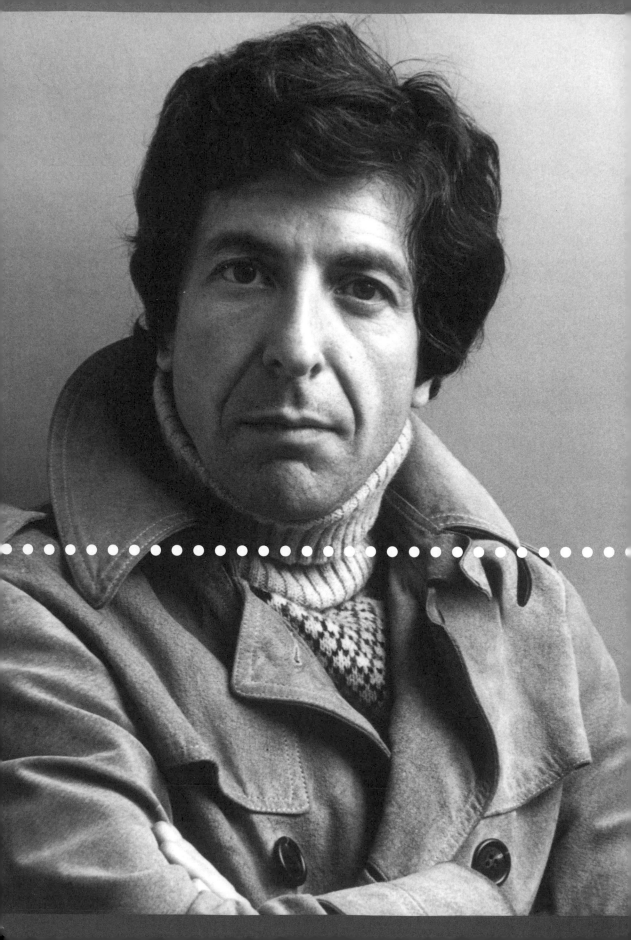

1934

Leonard Cohen born September 21 in Montreal. As a teenager he learns to play guitar and becomes fascinated by the poetry of Federico Garcia Lorca.

1961

The Spice-Box Of Earth published.

1960

Moves to the Greek island of Hydra.

1963

The Favorite Game published.

1951

Starts at McGill University.

1955

Graduates from McGill University.

1957

Leaves Columbia University.

1956

Starts at Columbia University.
Let Us Compare Mythologies published.

1964

Flowers For Hitler published.

1966

Moves to USA.

Parasites Of Heaven and *Beautiful Losers* published.

Judy Collins records two Leonard Cohen songs, 'Suzanne' and 'Dress Rehearsal Rag' on her *In My Life* album, thus introducing Cohen to a wide audience.

1971

Songs Of Love And Hate released.

1972

Son Adam born.

The Energy Of Slaves published.

1968

Selected Poems 1956-1968 published.

1974

Daughter Lorca born.

New Skin For The Old Ceremony released.

1970

Cohen tours for the first time, with dates in the United States, Canada and Europe, a highlight being his appearance before over 500,000 fans at the Isle of Wight Festival in the UK.

1967

Songs Of Leonard Cohen released.

1969

Songs From A Room released.

1994

Moves into the Mount Baldy Zen Center in California to begin five years of seclusion.

1979

Recent Songs released.

1991

Cohen is made an Officer of the Order of Canada.

1977

Death Of A Ladies' Man, produced by Phil Spector, released.

1988

I'm Your Man released.

2001

Ten New Songs released.

1978

Death Of A Lady's Man published.

1992

The Future released.

1984

Book Of Mercy published.

Various Positions released.

1999

Leaves Mount Baldy.

2003

Cohen is made a Companion to the Order of Canada, the country's highest civilian honour recognizing a lifetime of outstanding achievement, dedication to the community and service to the nation.

2004

Dear Heather released.

2006

Book Of Longing published.

2009

On 18 September Cohen collapses on stage at a concert in Valencia, Spain, halfway through performing 'Bird On The Wire'. He is admitted to local hospital with stomach problems, and possibly food poisoning. Three days later, on his 75th birthday, he performs in Barcelona, his last in Europe in 2009 and rumoured to be his last European concert ever.

2008

World Tour, his first in 15 years, begins. His performance at the Glastonbury Festival in June is acclaimed by many as the highlight of the event.

A version of 'Hallelujah' by Alexandra Burke tops the UK singles chart, becoming the fastest-selling single by a female artist in UK chart history. So much interest in the song is generated that Jeff Buckley's rendition occupies the number two spot while Cohen's original version enters the singles chart at 34, his first-ever British Top 40 single. With versions of the song holding down three Top 40 UK Singles Chart positions simultaneously, 'Hallelujah' became the fastest-selling digital single in European history.

2010

World Tour ends after 246 shows in Europe, Australia, Israel, Canada and the US.

2012

Old Ideas released.

INT

"Music to slit your wrists by". This easy joke about Leonard Cohen's work contains, like all good jokes, a seed of truth, but it is a seed that grows into a rather puny plant. Cohen is an intelligent and serious man as, in large part, is his audience. It would therefore be surprising if he had chosen to ignore the complexities of human existence and confined himself to rose-tinted niceties. As a consequence, and sometimes for more personal reasons, he has often painted a bleak picture of the world. What is important to note is that this is not all he has painted: all of Cohen's work exhibits a high standard of artistry, and everything he has done – good, bad or indifferent – has been done with conscious integrity.

The music of Leonard Cohen, which is described song-by-song in this book, offers a range of pleasures. He is first and foremost a very good songwriter. He has a gift for phraseology, which never comes without a love and knowledge of words. He has a command of form, which offers serious enjoyment for the connoisseur. He also possesses an often underrated talent for melody and has developed, in the studio and on tour, a solid musicianship.

RODUCTION

As a songwriter, Cohen has dealt with a wide variety of subjects, but there are consistent themes that run throughout his work. If there is one dominant theme it is love, though he has covered many different aspects of this universal, not to say infinite, subject. Many of his songs deal with the failure of relationships. In others, he is lyrical about carnal love. But he has also treated the subject of love more philosophically, assessing its importance as "the only engine of survival".

Another major theme in the work of Leonard Cohen is the tension between our need for freedom and the difficulties freedom can bring. He knows the pain of freedom just as much as the pain of confinement, and is well acquainted with existential fear. Although not an explicitly political writer, and rarely a direct social commentator, Cohen is clearly in the libertarian camp and on the side of social justice.

There is also a strong religious sensibility informing his work, founded in his native Judaism and consolidated by the Buddhism he has adopted in adult life. He remains a poet, however, not a theologian. It is the spiritual quest, the understanding of humankind's place in the cosmos, that interests Cohen, rather than rites of worship or definitions of divinity. His religious sensibility also enables him to utilise religious phraseology in songs with entirely secular subjects. (Curiously, many of his most spiritual songs avoid overtly religious language.)

Cohen is also witty – often wryly humorous. Listening to his music is, it must be stressed, an enjoyable experience. Though the world at large may perceive him as the "poet laureate of pessimism", the body of work he has produced is rewarding to encounter and offers gourmet pleasures to the discerning palate.

This book provides a guided tour of Leonard Cohen's musical output, through the ups and downs of his professional, commercial and personal life, from his earliest recordings to his most recent. Like any guided tour, it is intended to illuminate, to distinguish the major from the minor, and to point out obscure and interesting details. I hope you find it succeeds.

Leonard Cohen recorded his first album in 1967. Since then he has released a further 11 studio albums, six live albums and three volumes of "greatest hits". By any standards, this represents a long career and, in qualitative if perhaps not quantitative terms, a productive one, but it was not Cohen's

first. He is unusual, if not unique, in having established a considerable (though unremunerative) reputation as a poet and novelist before turning professionally to music. Some knowledge of Cohen's literary career and personal background would seem appropriate here, to facilitate an understanding of his music.

Cohen was born in Montreal in 1934 into a prosperous and respectable Jewish family. In his parents we can see the meeting of two distinct and typical threads in the tapestry of modern Jewish experience. His father's family had first arrived in Canada in 1869. His grandfather, Lyon Cohen, was a successful businessman, the head of the largest clothing manufacturers in the British Empire, as well as being a pillar of the Canadian Jewish community and an influential figure in political circles. He was a typical example of the outward-looking, cultured, English-speaking Jew referred to, in the fashionable phrase of the time, as "a gentleman of Hebrew persuasion".

His maternal grandfather, by contrast, embodied a different but equally representative Jewish experience. Rabbi Solomon Klinitsky-Klein was a Yiddish-speaking rabbinic scholar who had known, and fled, the pogroms in Eastern Europe. He and his young family did not arrive in Canada till 1923. An intellectual with a deep knowledge of the Talmud, Rabbi Klein was the kind of scholar of whom it was said that he could put a pin through a sacred tome and know every letter it touched. He had a profound influence on his grandson, both by exemplifying the erudite, devout yet poetic world of the ghetto rabbinate and by providing, through his final sad dementia, an early lesson about the nature of change and decay.

From 1951 to 1955, Cohen studied at Montreal's prestigious McGill University, where he fell into the company of poets and novelists. After graduating, and with two creative writing prizes under his belt, he resolved to follow a literary career. "I yearned", he later said, "to live a bohemian life; an unstructured life but a consecrated one". His motives may have been mixed (he has subsequently admitted that, "mostly what I was trying to do was get a date") but there is no doubt that he took writing seriously. He was one of a number of writers who saw themselves as an avant-garde dedicated to revitalising a Canadian literary scene that had become tame and bourgeoisified, "forced to write with maple syrup on birch bark" in Aileen Collins' evocative phrase. He wanted his own poems "to be informed by a sensibility which comprehends the bombing of cities, concentration camps and human infidelity". In that, he was a child of his time.

He travelled, living for a while in New York (where he hung out on the fringes of the emerging Beat scene and met the poet Allen Ginsberg) and London (where he mixed in West Indian circles and met the Black Muslim leader Michael X). In 1960 he bought a house on the Greek island of Hydra, where a small colony of writers and artists had established itself. By 1966, he had published four volumes of poetry (*Let Us Compare Mythologies, The Spice-Box Of Earth, Flowers For Hitler* and *Parasites Of Heaven*) and two novels (*The Favorite Game* and *Beautiful Losers*), but despite his burgeoning reputation he could not make the literary life pay for itself. Concluding that "poetry is no substitute for survival", he changed tack and started in earnest on a musical career.

There had long been a musical dimension to Cohen's life. He had bought his first guitar at fifteen. At summer camp, he had been introduced by left-wing friends to *The People's Songbook*. A year later, he wrote his first song – abandoned when he realised that he had inadvertently plagiarised a popular hit of the day. At McGill, he had formed a short-lived Country & Western combo called The Buckskin Boys. In 1958, he had given a poetry reading backed by a dozen or more jazz musicians. Music may have been a new departure professionally, but it was also an old friend.

It was as a songwriter rather than a performer that Cohen began his musical career. His earliest champion, the folksinger Judy Collins, included two Cohen songs ('Suzanne' and 'Dress Rehearsal Rag') on her 1966 album *In My Life*. On *Wildflowers* the following year, she covered three more – 'Sisters Of Mercy', 'Hey, That's No Way To Say Goodbye' and 'Priests', the latter a song Cohen has never recorded himself. Noel Harrison, later famous for his hit 'The Windmills Of Your Mind', also recorded 'Suzanne' and had a modest hit with it.

With Collins' encouragement, Cohen started singing in public. His first major performance came at a Benefit Concert in New York. Her encouragement on this occasion was crucial. The story goes that, after a few bars of 'Suzanne' and with his guitar detuned by the temperature drop when he got on stage, Cohen panicked and came off. Collins persuaded him to retune his guitar and go back on. Metaphorically at least, he has stayed on ever since.

The story of Leonard Cohen's recording career unfolds in the pages that follow. In parallel with his recording career, Cohen has also toured widely (curiously, he has played more gigs in Germany than anywhere else) and continued writing (six more volumes of his poetry - including two selections - have appeared since 1967). These activities are, however, outside the scope of this volume.

I cannot end without acknowledging the crucial role that Chris Allen has played in the writing of this book. It is literally true that I would not have been able to write it without the deep and sustaining relationship I have with him.

Maurice Ratcliff, London, 2012

PART I
STUDIO
ALBUMS

SONGS OF LEONARD COHEN

(First issued February 1968)

In 1967 Leonard Cohen was invited to lunch with the legendary producer John Hammond (whose discoveries included Billie Holliday, Bob Dylan and, later, Bruce Springsteen). After lunch, Cohen played him half a dozen of his songs. Hammond's judgement was terse but encouraging: "You got it, Leonard". Within a week, Cohen was in Columbia's 'E' studio in New York recording his first album.

Hammond himself was the original producer but he was forced to withdraw because of illness. His replacement was John Simon – an experienced producer with whom, perhaps unsurprisingly, the neophyte Cohen often argued. "CBS tried to make my songs into music; I got put down all the time," Cohen has said, but in fact he was still finding himself in the unfamiliar world of the studio. Simon certainly indulged him – recording him by candlelight in an incense-laden atmosphere and importing a mirror (Cohen had always played in front of one when practising at home) to put the new boy at ease.

Cohen's later verdict that Simon was "truly magnificent" seems a fairer judgement. That they disagreed on aesthetic questions ("I did not want drums on 'Suzanne'," Cohen complained) is not only unsurprising but, in the context of any creative activity, natural and inevitable. If the arrangements were Simon's, the final mix was undoubtedly Cohen's.

In any event, the resulting album presents Cohen's songs in a clear and limpid way, offering a classic example of Cohen's work as a singer-songwriter. In these songs we can see most of his principal themes already in play – love, loss and loneliness are expressed in accessible yet poetic language, and supported by simple yet memorable melodies. Alongside *Songs From A Room*, his début represents the apex of Cohen's achievement in the early period of his musical career.

Songs Of Leonard Cohen was unofficially released on 26 December 1967, although its official release date came the following year. It was a modest hit and prefigured Cohen's later career by proving more popular in Europe than in North America – it reached number 13 in the UK but only number 162 in the USA. A remastered edition of the album was released in 2007 which contained two previously unissued bonus tracks: 'Store Room' and 'Blessed Is The Memory'.

SUZANNE

'Suzanne' is probably Cohen's most famous song. It is the first song on his first album, appears on his most recent live album (*Songs From The Road*) and has been widely covered. Cohen himself has performed it on every one of his tours. And as if to symbolise his induction into showbiz, the publishing rights to it were ripped off (though Cohen has since bought them back).

The song is based on an earlier poem, 'Suzanne Takes You Down', from *Parasites Of Heaven*. Cohen has referred to it as "reportage", and it is comparatively rare among his songs in its references to real people, events and places. The Suzanne of the title (Suzanne Vaillancourt née Verdal, not Suzanne Elrod, the mother of his children Lorca and Adam) was a friend from Montreal. She was in the habit of serving a tea, sold by the name of Constant Comment, which is flavoured with orange rind ("she feeds you tea and oranges / That come all the way from China"), and the first verse sketches her character and Cohen's close but platonic relationship with her.

The second verse is imbued with the atmosphere of Montreal. Its religious variety (the Anglos are Protestant, the French-speaking majority are Catholic, and there is a significant Jewish population) is reflected in Cohen's homogenised – and somewhat original – theology ("And Jesus was a sailor"). The "lonely wooden tower" is the chapel of Nôtre Dame de Bon Secours, the mariners' church in old Montreal which features a figure of the Virgin ("our lady of the harbour") facing out to sea to bless departing ships. The third verse continues in similar vein, and introduces a theme to which Cohen would often return – the search for what he has elsewhere called the "compassionate attention that a man looks to receive from a woman".

Cohen's voice is soft and delicate, and well counterpointed by the higher register backing vocal provided, apparently, by John Simon's girlfriend. (Simon's own piano playing did not survive the mixing process.) A delicately picked guitar defines the melody, embellished by a subtle bass growl and lush strings. In short, a haunting version of a classic song, and one that announced the arrival of an original and distinctive voice.

MASTER SONG

Again based on a poem from *Parasites Of Heaven* ('I Believe I Heard Your Master Sing... '), this was another song whose publishing rights Cohen temporarily lost. At 5:54, 'Master Song' is the longest song on the album. The song tells of a philosophically complicated, and not fully explained, *ménage à trois* (between the singer, his woman and her "master"), a theme that Cohen had explored in his novel *Beautiful Losers*. The accompanying rhythm guitar is somewhat repetitive and needs the variation provided by the electronically-distorted instruments that punctuate the song.

The portrait of the master who appears to have cuckolded the singer is far from flattering. It is curious to note that not long after recording *Songs Of Leonard Cohen*, he met his own 'master' – Joshu Sasaki (known as Roshi) – in whose Zen Buddhist monastery in California he later lived and who, unlike the

"master" in this song, is not known to have "failed". It is perhaps no coincidence that 'Master Song' has not figured in the set-list on any of Cohen's tours.

WINTER LADY

Although addressed to one woman (the "travelling lady" whom he asks to "stay awhile until the night is over"), 'Winter Song' is in fact about another who, unlike the first, really is his lover. This is a different kind of triangle from the one in 'Master Song'. Whatever his intentions towards the woman in his presence (and they may be easily guessed), it is the absent woman who occupies his thoughts. There are clear echoes of Cohen's then fading relationship with the Norwegian model Marianne Ihlen – "Well, I lived with a child of snow / When I was a soldier / And I fought every man for her / Until the nights grew colder". The view of male-female relationships as a battlefield and the sense of his own war-weariness are eloquently and poignantly expressed. The song was later used on the soundtrack of Robert Altman's film *McCabe & Mrs Miller*.

THE STRANGER SONG

'The Stranger Song' is one of Cohen's earliest songs; he had been singing it for at least two years before he recorded it. It is not, grammatically at least, a song in which he himself is a protagonist – verses 7 and 8 need to be read, like other uses of the word "I" in the song, as reported speech. However, despite its third-person language, the world-weary tone is authentically Cohen's own. A number of phrases ("He wants to trade the game he plays for shelter" or "You hate to watch another tired man / Lay down his hand / Like he was giving up the holy game of poker") can be read as metaphors for Cohen's abandonment, as he would have seen it at the time, of literary ambitions for the 'shelter' of music.

The Stranger's disclaimer that "I never had a secret chart / To get me to the heart of this / Or any other matter" might be Cohen's own confession. The wonderful line "He was just some Joseph looking for a manger" (i.e. an ordinary man doing what he has to in ignorance of its wider significance) can be seen in the same light. It is also a good example of a literary device that Cohen has often employed - the use of traditional religious images or vocabulary for non-religious purposes.

'The Stranger Song' was also used on the *McCabe & Mrs Miller* soundtrack. Indeed, some regard the whole film as, in the words of Jim Devlin, "the perfect two-hour promo video for this song".

SISTERS OF MERCY

'Sisters Of Mercy' was the third track from the album to be used on the soundtrack of *McCabe & Mrs Miller*. The equally famous story of its origins is best told in Cohen's own words.

"I was in Edmonton, doing a tour by myself, I guess this was around '67, and I was walking along one of the main streets of Edmonton. It was bitter cold and I knew no-one. I passed these two girls in a doorway and they invited me to stand in the doorway with them. Of course I did, and sometime later we found ourselves in my little hotel room, and the three of us were going to go to sleep together. Of course I had all kinds of erotic fantasies about what the evening might bring. We went to bed together, all jammed into this one small couch in this little hotel, and it became clear that wasn't the purpose of the evening at all, and at one point in the night I found myself unable to sleep.

"I got up and by the moonlight, it was very very bright and the moon was being reflected off the snow, and I wrote that poem by the ice-reflected moonlight while these women were sleeping. It was one of the few songs I ever wrote from top to bottom without a line of revision. The words flowed and the melody flowed. By the time they woke up the next morning, it was dawn. I had this completed song to sing to them."

That the girls' names were Barbara and Lorraine is, of course, entirely irrelevant.

SO LONG, MARIANNE

This beautiful song took Cohen over a year to write, and reflects the end-game of his relationship with Marianne Ihlen. Cohen later said of the song that, "I didn't think I was saying goodbye but I guess I was". In fact, the song's overt subject is the need to redefine a relationship – "it's time we began / To laugh and cry and cry and laugh about it all again".

The song contains some wonderful phraseology: the line "We met when we were almost young" has the shiver of authentic poetry. It also touches on some of Cohen's perennial themes: loneliness ("Your letters they all say that you're beside me now / Then why do I feel alone?"), freedom, and existential fear ("You left when I told you I was curious / I never said that that I was brave"). Musically, the soft timbre of Cohen's voice contrasts most effectively with the harsher tones of the female backing vocalists. And is it too fanciful to detect in the drum's almost military tattoo an echo of the lover-as-soldier image used in 'Winter Lady'?

HEY, THAT'S NO WAY TO SAY GOODBYE

This tender elegy on the theme of lovers parting is a slight but perfectly realised song. No-one who has known the joy of physical love will fail to recognise the *mise-en-scène* with which it opens: "I loved you in the morning / Our kisses deep and warm / Your hair upon the pillow / Like a sleepy golden storm". The effect is enhanced by the simplicity of the backing – just a guitar and a Jew's harp, with a sharp yet warm female voice echoing the "hey" of the title line.

Thematically, there is some similarity between this song and 'So Long, Marianne'. Both deal with departure. Both suggest the relationship in question is at, or coming to, an end. In terms of the structure of the album, this counterpoint is artistically useful, but the story of the song's genesis underlines the perils of reading too much autobiographical detail into a work of art. 'Hey, That's No Way To Say Goodbye' is not factually about Cohen's relationship with Marianne. The song was written in 1966 in New York's Penn Terminal Hotel and was inspired by another woman entirely. According to Cohen, "I was with the wrong woman as usual". Marianne was reportedly less than impressed when she came across a rough draft of the song in his notebook.

STORIES OF THE STREET

This bleak song, in the words of Cohen's biographer Ira B. Nadel, "documents (his) despair and dislocation during his early days in New York". It opens descriptively ("The Spanish voices laugh / The Cadillacs go creeping now / Through the night and the poison gas"), but it is not really a reportage song. It is too personal, too desperate, for that – and one might add that it seems too little distilled from the raw experience on which it is based to succeed in transmuting Cohen's individual pain into poetry.

Pain the song certainly contains, but it is a self-indulgent pain. One does not need too much knowledge of the world's suffering to wonder if the problems of freedom or the 'age of lust' are quite in the premier division. "You are locked into your suffering and your pleasures are the seal" the singer observes – one suspects that Cohen is talking to himself. When he requests that, should he "Wake at night and wonder who I am", he will be taken "to the slaughterhouse / I will lie there with the lamb", it is hard to avoid the suspicion that the lamb appears less for its religious symbolism than because it is a convenient rhyme. It may be no coincidence that 'Stories of the Street' is another track which has never been included in Cohen's touring repertoire.

TEACHERS

'Teachers' is the third song on the album based on a poem ('I Met A Woman Long Ago') from *Parasites Of Heaven*. Its subject matter is, as Dorman and Rawlins put it it in *Prophet Of the Heart* (Omnibus Press, 1990), the "spurious gurus who take everything, negate everything, disrupt and ruin others' lives – and leave their victims

puzzled and empty". "Have I carved enough, my Lord?" the singer asks; "Child, you are a bone" is the discouraging reply.

The song is thematically similar to 'Master Song' and takes a similarly jaundiced view of the self-appointed 'teachers of my heart'. Musically it is somewhat monotonous, and it is not a song Cohen has persisted with. Its only known live performance was on BBC TV in the summer of 1968.

ONE OF US CANNOT BE WRONG

This elegantly crafted song with its simple, pretty guitar accompaniment has an inelegant and ugly subject. "I lit a thin green candle / To make you jealous of me" the song opens, but it is clear that the singer's own jealousy is the dominant emotion. His confession that he "Tortured the dress / That you wore for the world to see through" is a skilful piece of writing, combining self-knowledge with insult, pain with bile. Despite his lover's infidelity – with the Doctor, the Saint and the Eskimo, all of whom seem to have suffered at least as much as he has – the singer ends by begging her to return to him. "You stand there so nice / In your blizzard of ice / Oh please let me come into the storm". No unhappy lover will fail to recognise the emotion in that plea.

The final moments of the song offer an interesting insight into Cohen's craftsmanship. A series of sweet "la-la-las" transmute into an anguished scream, and show how consciously he is using the medium of song. Within the piece he is expressing emotion for sure, but as the artist standing outside and 'controlling' the work he lets us know that he knows, and has anatomised, exactly what is going on. The emotion is not raw but cooked. It is a fine and revealing ending to an impressive first album. Cohen has performed 'One Of Us Cannot Be Wrong' on every tour to date, which suggests that he has a very clear understanding of the song's quality.

SONGS FROM A ROOM

(First issued April 1969)

Cohen decided to record his second album in Nashville. Although Nashville's mainstream product – Dolly Parton, Merle Haggard, et al – was far removed in style and attitude from the 'counter-culture' of rock and folk with which Cohen was commercially and spiritually allied, there was a high standard of musicianship in the C&W capital. (Bob Dylan had recently recorded *John Wesley Harding* and *Nashville Skyline* there.) In going to Nashville, Cohen was to some extent going with the flow of fashion – both musically and by "getting it together in the country" in the cabin he rented from the legendary Everly Brothers songsmith Boudleaux Bryant. At the same time, Cohen had long had a genuine affection for country music, witness his first band The Buckskin Boys.

His new producer, Bob Johnston, was an old Nashville hand who had worked with Dylan, Johnny Cash and Simon & Garfunkel among others. He was also no mean pianist and would later join Cohen's touring band, The Army. *Songs From A Room* was recorded in Columbia's newly refitted studio on 16th Avenue. Stylistically, it was similar to *Songs Of Leonard Cohen*, being a classic 'singer with guitar' record. Its production was spare, using no drums and only limited electric guitar. Thematically, it continued in the direction set by his first album – the perils of love and the problems of freedom were still the principal diet on which Cohen's imagination fed.

Songs From A Room was released in the spring of 1969. On the back cover was a photo of Marianne sitting in the eponymous room in Cohen's house on Hydra. This is not a little ironic, given that they had split up the previous year (Cohen was now living with Suzanne Elrod) and that much of the writing had been done in California. The album was a success, reaching number 2 in the UK charts and winning a Canadian gold disc though, in the by now familiar pattern, it was less successful in the USA. Its popularity in France – where President Pompidou was reputedly a fan – led to Cohen being named "le folksinger de l'année" by *Le Nouvel Observateur*. Most Cohen fans would agree that *Songs From A Room* is Cohen's best album, at least from his early period.

The album was reissued in 2007 with two bonus tracks - previously unreleased and clearly earlier versions of 'Bird On The Wire' (here titled 'Like A Bird') and 'You Know Who I Am' ('Nothing To One'). It is interesting to hear them in that they give a glimpse of how the songs developed during the recording process, but it is also obvious why the takes released on the original album were chosen.

 ### BIRD ON THE WIRE

This is undoubtedly a classic Cohen song. The themes of freedom ("I have tried in my way to be free") and infidelity ("If I have been untrue / I hope you know it was never to you") are core subjects in his work. In the sublime couplets of the second chorus ("I saw a beggar leaning on his wooden crutch / He said to me 'you must ask for so much' / And a pretty woman leaning in her darkened door / She cried to me 'Hey, why not ask for more?' ") the tension between the constraints imposed by life's suffering and the ambitions that freedom permits – a tension that informs so much of Cohen's work – is eloquently and poetically presented.

The title image – which it must be admitted is not immediately accessible – derives from an event on Hydra. Shortly after Cohen arrived there, the island's first telegraph wires were installed. The birds soon began to use them as a perch. "I would stare out of the window," Cohen has said "and think how civilisation had caught up with me and I wasn't going to be able to... live this eleventh-century life that I had found for myself. So that was the beginning".

The slow spare treatment and the world-weary voice make this a definitive version of the song. Indeed, it is not too fanciful to see it as Cohen's equivalent of Frank Sinatra's 'My Way'; 'Bird On The Wire' is certainly stylistically representative of Cohen's work, and offers a concise expression of his world-view. Frequently used to open his live shows ("It seems to return me to my duties"), and ever-present on tour, it has become something of a Cohen anthem. It is therefore surprising that Cohen has revised the lyrics so often – as early as 1972, the version later included on *Live Songs* differs in many respects, and further changes are present in later live performances.

STORY OF ISAAC

Based on the biblical story of Abraham and Isaac, this song, Cohen tells us, "says something about fathers and sons and that curious place, generally over the slaughtering block, where generations meet and have their intercourse". The song is not personally autobiographical – his father had died when Cohen was a boy, before any personal or philosophical conflicts could develop. Nor, despite the biblical resonance of its narrative, does the song really deal with the conflict between the contemporary Cohen and the Jewish tradition his father had bequeathed him.

In a more general sense, however, the song reflects a conflict in which Cohen surely saw himself engaged – the conflict between the ideas of the emerging counter-culture, specifically its demands for social and sexual freedom, and the hide-bound traditions of mainstream North American culture. Cohen's position is clearly stated: "you who build the altars now / to sacrifice these children / you

must not do it anymore". In an echo of his earlier avant-garde critique of the unimaginative Canadian literary scene, he tells his cultural adversaries, "A scheme is not a vision / You never have been tempted / By a demon or a god". In stating this clear preference for the visionary over the mundane, Cohen nails his colours firmly to the counter-cultural mast.

A BUNCH OF LONESOME HEROES

This is another song which cannibalises an earlier poem, the third verse having appeared as the second verse of 'New Poem' in *Selected Poems, 1956-1968*. It is easy to concur with Stephen Scobie that it "remains intriguing but inconclusive". Although one of the heroes wants "to tell my story / Before I turn into gold" (not, it must be said, a common risk that story-tellers run), does not vouchsafe what his story is. His dedication – "I sing this for the crickets / I sing this for the army / I sing this for your children / And for all who do not heed me" – smacks more of cleverness than of a serious attempt to define his audience.

For all its insubstantiality, however, the song does exude an atmosphere of "outsiderhood" that would have touched a contemporary nerve. Recorded with a basic guitar-and-bass backing, enhanced by kazoo-like electronic distortion, it does convey a sense of heroic defiance that seems, today, rather of its time. Unsurprisingly, there are no reports of this song ever having been sung in public.

THE PARTISAN

'The Partisan' was the first song Cohen recorded that he did not write himself. The original was written in 1944, in French, by Anna Marly, who ran a hostel for French exiles in London. Hy Zaret (better known for 'Unchained Melody') translated it into English. The version Cohen sings is substantially Zaret's, although verse two is omitted, with this verse and the following two being sung in French at the end. There are some interesting if minor differences between the French and English versions. "Les Allemands" become the more neutral "soldiers". The shelter-giving "old woman" is "un vieux homme" in the original.

Cohen had originally come across 'The Partisan' in *The People's Songbook* as a young man at summer camp. It is a rare excursion for him into political territory, although the generality of the lyrics translates the story into one about a more generic exile, one more akin to the cultural or spiritual exile that his other songs explore than to the social and political exile of the *maquisard*.

This version is very effectively delivered, with a plodding bass line underpinning the simply strummed guitar and an occasional accordion adding additional (and appropriate) colour. The vocals which back Cohen during the French verses are reported to have been overdubbed during a trip Cohen and Johnston made to France in search of 'authenticity'.

SEEMS SO LONG AGO, NANCY

A reportage song, the basic story concerns a Montreal friend of Cohen's, the daughter of a judge, whose free and promiscuous life ("Nancy wore green stockings / And she slept with everyone") ended in suicide ("a .45 beside her head / An open telephone"). Others have stated that the facts of the case are not entirely as Cohen presents them in his song, but it is the poet's task to digest rather than to report facts. The subject is chosen for its resonance with some of Cohen's favourite themes – alienation and the existential terror of freedom.

Hauntingly recorded, with a slow and sparsely embellished accompaniment to Cohen's mournful singing (and does he have a slight problem hitting the song's highest notes?), 'Nancy' ends on a suitably ambiguous note: "In the hollow of the night / When you are cold and numb / You hear her talking freely then / She's happy that you've come." Leaving aside the sexual connotations of "come" (with its echoes of post-coital tristesse and of orgasm as the "little death"), are we to conclude that her ghost's happiness derives from the misery of the living or that, having already explored the *terra incognita* of death, her example makes it unnecessary for others to follow her? Cohen is nothing if not a poet, and poets thrive on ambiguity. It is for his audience to find the song's meaning.

THE OLD REVOLUTION

Just as 'Story Of Isaac' uses the language of religion but does not have a directly spiritual theme, so 'The Old Revolution' uses the language of politics but does not address social issues. I have to confess that I cannot discern what exactly it does address. There is some wonderful phraseology ("even damnation is poisoned with rainbows") and some clever inversions ("I finally broke into the prison"), and the tone is knowing and disillusioned. But what is the protagonist talking about, and why? Ambiguity is all very well, but it seems that here Cohen has strayed over the boundary into imprecision, that he has indeed "started to stutter / As though (he) had nothing to say". For all that, the song *feels* as though it is chock full of meaning, and enough fans must have thought so for it was reasonably successful when released as a single. Nonetheless, Cohen has not chosen to play it live.

THE BUTCHER

This is another song that does not easily yield up its meaning. It has been claimed that it is a song about drugs, doubtless because the singer "found a silver needle (and) put it into my arm". It is a matter of record that Cohen took drugs at this point in his life (marijuana and Mandrax appear to have been his main tastes, and there is a famous story of him collapsing in the street after eating opium with the fugitive Scottish novelist and 'public junkie' Alexander Trocchi). But if 'The Butcher' is a song about drugs then it is a peculiarly obscure treatment of the subject.

The key to the song must be the butcher's slaughter of the lamb. If we take the lamb as symbolising personal (and perhaps cultural) innocence and simplicity, then the song's subject matter becomes clearer. It is society's spiritual murder of the pure and innocent that Cohen is dealing with. The use of the needle in the second verse is thus not a personal confession, but the description of one route – towards oblivion – that offers an escape from the negative cultural condition of the times. If we remember the attitude of Cohen and his literary confrères to the prevailing culture in Montreal in the Fifties, then we can see 'The Butcher' as simply another station on a road he had long been travelling.

 ### YOU KNOW WHO I AM

With 'You Know Who I Am', Cohen returns to the narrower confines of a personal relationship. The song is clearly addressed to a woman, though it is the singer's character and characteristics – not hers – that are delineated. This limits the song. It is a good rule of poetry to avoid writing about "I", the danger being that the writer becomes ego-bound and unable to generalise his individual experience so as to make it interesting and relevant to others. Cohen seems to fall into this trap here. His need (to see her "naked" or "wild") may be pressing, but he does little to discourage us from saying "so what?" That he sometimes needs her "to kill a child" is selfish if it refers to abortion, and frankly obscene otherwise. His self-description as "the one who loves changing from nothing to one" comes perilously close to claiming divine characteristics. All in all, an unappetisingly immature song.

 ### LADY MIDNIGHT

At first sight a deceptively simple story of successful seduction – it starts with the singer going "by myself to a very crowded place" and ends with the woman he meets there telling him "you've won me, you've won me, my lord" – it is on closer inspection a much more complex tale. Who is Lady Midnight? Is she a real woman or a symbol? Does she represent the "dark night of the soul" or is she Death itself? And does the "sweet early morning" through which the singer walks at the end of the song signify a victory over the darkness or a surrender to it? Reader, judge for yourself.

TONIGHT WILL BE FINE

Cohen has written few if any simple and uncomplicated love songs like, for instance, Bob Dylan's 'Lay Lady Lay', but this song comes closest. The melody is tuneful and friendly, the tone seductive, the chorus – rarely for Cohen – repeats a simple, happy phrase: "tonight will be fine, will be fine, will be fine, will be fine... ". Then comes the sting in the tail: "... for a while".

Cohen has acknowledged 'Tonight Will Be Fine' as the first proper song he wrote, and it contains many elements that he would rework throughout his career – the sensual and elegiac tone, the failing relationship, the rainbow moments seized in the face of damnation. Here he shoulders all the blame for the relationship's failure himself: "You went right on loving / I went on a fast". He also provides what is by all accounts a faithful description of his domestic aesthetic. "I choose the rooms / That I live in with care / The windows are small / And the walls almost bare / There's only one bed / And only one..." – here he sings "prayer" where the listener expects "chair". This expectation is probably accurate from an interior design perspective, but the unexpected shift is a good example of the experienced poet at work at the beginning of his songwriting career. Apart from hitting the rhyme – a merely technical requirement – he achieves surprise (always a useful effect) and also leads us into and enhances the significance of the next line, "I listen all night for your foot on the stair".

As with *Songs Of Leonard Cohen*, the album ends with Cohen singing non-verbally. This time however the tone is sweeter and less anguished, which makes the anguish that informs the rest of the album all the more poignant. As he takes his leave, the artist is whistling in the dark to keep up his existential courage.

SONGS OF LOVE AND HATE

(First issued March 1971)

For his third album, Cohen retained the services of Bob Johnston as producer and again recorded it mainly in Nashville – this time in Columbia's 'A' studio. Recording began in March 1970, 'Avalanche' being the first track laid down. Progress was, however, not as smooth as hitherto. Cohen has confessed to the depression and negativity he was suffering at this period of his life. "Absolutely everything was beginning to fall apart around me: my spirit, my intentions, my will... I began to believe all the negative things people said about my way of singing. I began to hate the sound of my voice." The album was more or less finished by the November. Cohen then went on the road, taking the opportunity to try out his new songs live. After the tour, he flew to London to work with the respected arranger Paul Buckmaster, overdubbing strings and horns on several tracks. The voices of the Corona Academy children's choir was also added to 'Last Year's Man' and 'Dress Rehearsal Rag'. At the last minute, a live version of 'Sing Another Song, Boys' was substituted for the studio cut. The album was finally finished in March 1971, a year after recording had begun.

Several musicians who had appeared on *Songs From A Room* were again featured on the new album – Charlie Daniels (bass, fiddle and acoustic guitar), Ron Cornelius (acoustic and electric guitar) and Bubba Fowler (banjo, bass and acoustic guitar). Bob Johnston played keyboards as well as fulfilling his producer's duties. Despite this continuity, however, the overall feel of the album is significantly different from *Songs Of Leonard Cohen* or *Songs From A Room*. The arrangements are fuller, with more of a rock'n'roll feel – in this sense looking forward to his future style rather than back to the 'singer with guitar' style he had previously adopted. Cohen's voice is harsher and more bitter, reflecting perhaps his bleaker personal feelings. Parts of the album Cohen himself found "a little burdened and melodramatic", adding that "I think that's the fault of the songs and the singer – it's a failure of that particular album but it's not a characteristic of the work" as a whole. As he often did, Cohen reworked several earlier songs and poems.

The working title *Leonard Cohen: Army* (the name he gave to his touring band) was changed to the more telling – and accurate – *Songs Of Love And Hate* for its release in the spring of 1971. Unlike his first two albums, it was not a commercial success. It did not go gold, even in Canada. Whether because of the change of style or the grimmer tone, Cohen's public did not follow the direction in which he was moving. It was to be more than a decade before he began to recapture the popularity he had known earlier.

A remastered version of the album was released in 2007 that included as a bonus track an early version of 'Dress Rehearsal Rag'.

AVALANCHE

 It is clear from the album's opening song that Cohen is in an ugly mood. The first sentence sets the tone – "I stepped into an avalanche / It covered up my soul". Both the "you" and the "I" characters are in pain, though the song's sympathy is clearly with "I" 's hurt – "Your pain is no credential here / It's just the shadow... of my wound" – and we can gauge Cohen's low self-esteem from the line "I myself am the pedestal for this ugly hump at which you stare".

The song is based on the poem 'I Stepped Into An Avalanche' from *Parasites Of*

Heaven. The arrangement is given a sinister ambience by the lush strings ('soggy' in Ken Tucker's opinion) overdubbed in London. "There is something in the voice" Cohen has remarked "that is really wiped out... it's a disturbing voice... there is anxiety there". One may conclude that this is indeed a 'song of hate'.

LAST YEAR'S MAN

 It was not a new departure for Cohen to sing about suffering, but there is a sense in this song that he is spiritually and emotionally becalmed, locked in the prison of himself, going nowhere, which is not found in his earlier work. "The skylight..." – a prison image par excellence – "... is like the skin / For a drum I'll never mend" he tells us twice. Again he uses religious terminology – Bethlehem, Babylon, Jesus, Cain – in a song that does not deal with explicitly religious themes, a feature perhaps of his personal desperation and an echo of the restless spiritual searching we know he was engaged on at the time. "We read from pleasant bibles / That are bound in blood and skin / That the wilderness is gathering all / Its children back again". Boy, is he hurting!

DRESS REHEARSAL RAG

 A song about suicide ("that's a funeral in the mirror"), 'Dress Rehearsal Rag' was one of Cohen's earliest songs; Judy Collins had covered it in 1966. Cohen performed it on BBC TV in 1968, introducing it thus: "There's a song in... Czechoslovakia called 'Gloomy Sunday' that [it] was forbidden to play because every time it would play people would leap out of windows... It was a tragic song... I have one of those songs that I have banned for myself – I sing it only on extremely joyous occasions when I know that the landscape can support the despair that I'm about to project into it". Apart from this recording, he is not known to have played it since, though he can have known few less joyous times than this period of his life.

DIAMONDS IN THE MINE

By contrast, Cohen has often played 'Diamonds In The Mine' in concert. Indeed, although this version is a studio recording, it has a distinctly live feel. Against a reggae-ish backing decorated with a fluid and lyrical electric guitar and sweet female voices, Cohen growls and swings his way through the splenetic lyrics. His throwaway comments ("You tell 'em now" he instructs the backing singers at the end of the second verse; "That's all I got to say" he advises the audience at the end) reflect his growing confidence and experience as a live performer.

Despite the "subterranean seam of condemnatory disgust" that Jim Devlin identifies in *In Every Style Of Passion* (Omnibus Press, 1997), there is a greater sense of fun in this than in his other 'songs of hate'. Perhaps the secret is that in this case Cohen is not writing directly about himself. There is no internal evidence from the song that he is involved with its subject, though the heat of his emotion does not suggest indifference. Nonetheless, the technical effect of his not personally being a character in the song is that Cohen is liberated from the danger of egocentricity he would otherwise face and can give free range to his verbal inventiveness. And what wonderful angry images of exhaustion he conjures: "There are no letters in the mailbox / And there are no grapes upon the vine / And there are no chocolates in your boxes any more / And there are no diamonds in the mine".

LOVE CALLS YOU BY YOUR NAME

After four 'songs of hate', Cohen allows himself a 'song of love'. Rewriting an unpublished 1967 song called 'Love Tries To Call You By Your Name', he offers at last a glimmer of hope, one that "you" (we may assume Cohen himself) "thought... could never happen". Once again – "here, right here" – love is a possibility. Lyrically, the most interesting feature of this song is the succession of pairs of things love is found "between". Cohen has set himself a difficult technical challenge by choosing to rhyme (or at least vowel-rhyme) them with the word "name" from the title line. Many of the pairs work well – "the darkness and the stage", "the moonlight and the lane", "the windmill and the grain". Others – "the peanuts and the cage", "the victim and his stain" – are more obscure, but yield their meaning after a little thought. One or two – "the sailboat and the drain", "the sundial and the chain" – have, I must confess, defeated me.

FAMOUS BLUE RAINCOAT

One of Cohen's most well-known songs, 'Famous Blue Raincoat' is also one of his most technically accomplished. Cast as a letter to a male friend who is clearly the third point of a romantic triangle involving 'my woman' Jane and Cohen himself, the form is expertly conveyed in a few epistolary phrases – "New York is cold but I like where I'm living", "Well, I see Jane's awake / She sends her regards" and the sign-off, "Sincerely, L. Cohen". Closer examination reveals the song to be rather more complex.

Cohen's sleevenotes for the *Greatest Hits* compilation offer an interesting clue: they are all about the "Burberry I got in London in 1959". His contemporary friends all report Cohen's attachment to this coat, even after it had become distressed and been repaired. Yet in the song it is the letter's addressee whose "famous blue raincoat was torn at the shoulder". Another clue can be found in the song's question "Did you ever go clear?". 'Going clear' is a term of art in Scientology, and we know Cohen was briefly involved in the Scientology movement in New York in 1968. Furthermore, having identified himself as the "I" character more clearly than in any other song, Cohen – an only son and obviously still alive – calls the other man "my brother, my killer".

Is it not a better reading of the song to suggest that Cohen is writing to himself or, more precisely, to a past self? If so, then the accusation that "You treated my woman to a flake of your life / And when she came back she was nobody's wife" is directed at himself. The song can now be seen as Cohen's shouldering of his own responsibility for the failure of his relationship(s). The "thin gypsy thief" is a self-portrait and the hope that "you're keeping some kind of record" is realised in the very song that expresses it.

SING ANOTHER SONG, BOYS

On 31 August 1970, Cohen and The Army, essentially the same musicians he was working with in the studio, played the 3rd Isle of Wight Festival (the 'Jimi Hendrix' one). The set comprised 'Bird On The Wire', 'So Long, Marianne', 'You Know Who I Am', 'Dead Song' (a poem – Cohen regularly recited poems during his concerts in those days), 'Lady Midnight', 'They Locked Up A Man' and 'A Person Who Eats Meat' (two more poems), 'One Of Us Cannot Be Wrong', 'The Stranger Song' (solo), 'Tonight Will Be Fine', 'Hey, That's No Way To Say Goodbye', 'Diamonds In The Mine', 'Suzanne', 'Sing Another Song, Boys', 'The Partisan', 'Famous Blue Raincoat' and 'Seems So Long Ago, Nancy'. The live Isle of Wight version of 'Sing Another Song, Boys' replaced the studio version just before Songs Of Love And Hate went to press. It was the first live version of a song that Cohen had released.

JOAN OF ARC

Songs Of Love And Hate begins with the icy frigidity of an avalanche; it ends in the flames of a funeral pyre. Cohen is no historian, nor does he pretend to be, and the student will glean no insight into the medieval French heroine of the Hundred Years War, the Maid of Orléans Jeanne d'Arc. Cohen's Joan is the product of his imagination, and his relationship with her is abstracted and poetical. There is no hint of domestic reality here, no documentary process. The consuming nature of his passion is nonetheless real enough – "and then she clearly understood, if he was fire, oh, then she was wood".

There are strong echoes in the song of Cohen's unrequited love for Nico, the German model, singer and Warhol acolyte whom he had met in New York. He has admitted that the song "came through her", and she was certainly "a cold and lonesome heroine". Unfortunately for Cohen, her tastes ran more to young men and narcotic oblivion than to thirty-something folksingers and intense relationships.

Technically, 'Joan Of Arc' finds Cohen in experimental mode. The four stanzas are sung and recited on overlapping tracks, giving the song an eerie and ethereal feeling that matches – and suits – the material. The idea derives from medieval palimpsests, manuscripts with new lines written over old. "I just thought it appropriate at that moment" he later said, and what further justification need be sought?

NEW SKIN FOR THE OLD CEREMONY

(First issued August 1974)

Cohen's fourth studio album was recorded in New York, in the Sound Ideas Studio. It was produced by John Lissauer, to whom Cohen had been introduced by Lewis Furey, a musician friend of his from Montreal who was to play viola on the album. Cohen had had some doubts about whether he would ever record another album. He had been unable to finish the songs he was working on and "thought for very good reasons the Muse had deserted me". His relationship with Suzanne Elrod was in trouble, despite the fact that she was pregnant with their daughter Lorca (who was born in September 1974 shortly after the album's release), and he was personally at a low ebb. Nonetheless, "for some reason I had a golden fortnight and a lot of songs presented conclusions to me".

The change of scene from Nashville to New York allowed (or necessitated) a wholesale change of personnel among his backing band. Moving away from the guitar, bass and Jew's harp sound that had typified his earlier work, *New Skin For The Old Ceremony* utilised a richer range of instruments – viola, banjo, mandolin, trumpet, woodwinds and percussion are credited along with the more familiar guitar, bass, keyboards and drums. His guru Roshi was invited to at least one session. (His advice that Cohen should "sing sadder" might strike some as falling into the 'coals to Newcastle' category.) Cohen was happy with

the results. "I must say I'm pleased with the album," he announced the following year. "I'm not ashamed of it and am ready to stand by it. Rather than think of it as a masterpiece, I prefer to think of it as a little gem." Despite attracting some critical acclaim, however, the album was not a commercial success, failing to make the US charts and achieving only moderate success in the UK, though it did better in continental Europe.

The album's artwork created some controversy. Based on the "symbolic representation of the *coniunctio spirituum*, or the spiritual union of the male and female principle" from a sixteenth-century alchemical text rediscovered by the psychologist C.G. Jung, it was felt to be too sexually explicit. In the UK, the angels' wings were re-drawn to conceal their genitalia, while in the USA the design was replaced by a photo of Cohen. The original artwork was restored when the album was re-issued on CD.

 IS THIS WHAT YOU WANTED
Once again, Cohen re-used a poem when writing a song. In this case, the chorus was taken from 'Poem number 31' in *The Energy Of Slaves*, though this was a more recent volume (1972) than he those he had previously recycled. "Is this what you wanted / To live in a house that is haunted / By the ghost of you and me?" he asks, positioning himself clearly at the heart of a moribund relationship.

The song has a much more bluesy feel than anything Cohen had done before, though the cracked growl of his voice is familiar from 'Diamonds In The Mine' on his previous album. The structure is simple, using a pattern that is something of a Cohen trademark – a series of different examples or images of the song's basic motif. Here, the pattern is based on "You were... ; I was ...", moving from the romantically flattering conjunction of "... the promise at dawn; ... the morning after" to the unromantically carnal conclusion ("you said you could never love me; I undid your gown") via the facetious ("... Jesus Christ my Lord; ... the moneylender"), the vulgar ("… the manual orgasm; … the dirty little boy") and the frankly bizarre ("… the whore and beast of Babylon; … Rin-Tin-Tin").

CHELSEA HOTEL number 2

'Chelsea Hotel number 1' was a slower version of this song, with different lyrics, which Cohen performed on his 1972 tour. The rewrite was completed during his visit to Ethiopia the following year, and has featured in his live act ever since. This rendition is a reversion to the simple 'singer plus guitar' style of his first two albums, and the sweet melancholy tone of his voice is equally familiar. The self-deprecating humour ("You told me again you preferred handsome men / But for me you would make an exception") underlines the song's fond and compassionate memories of the woman who "got away".

Cohen later revealed that the song derived from his affair with Janis Joplin, though he came to regret this ungallant indiscretion. It is, however, wrong to see 'Chelsea Hotel number 2' as simply a piece of autobiography. If that were so, the denouement ("I can't keep track of each fallen robin / … I don't think of you that often") would be too callous, and out of keeping with overall tone of the song. I think the song is better read as a hymn of praise to the freedom found in a simple, uncomplicated and 'pure' sexual encounter. The chorus makes the point: "You got away, I never once heard you say / 'I need you, I don't need you' / … and all of that jiving around". Surely the song's subject is not Janis Joplin but Suzanne Elrod, from whom we can be sure Cohen felt he was suffering a great deal of "jiving around".

LOVER LOVER LOVER

In 1973, as the storm clouds gathered that would eventually burst into the Yom Kippur War, Cohen visited Israel. His reasons were complex and personal – and he appears to have been in a sexually rampant mood throughout the trip – but they included a strong desire to help Israel in its battle with Egypt and "to make my atonement". He volunteered to serve, and was co-opted to entertain the troops in the Sinai desert, where this song was written.

Despite the circumstances of its creation and the lines "may the spirit of this song… /… be a shield for you… against the enemy", the song is not 'about' the war. Its theme is renovation, both of a relationship ("lover… come back to me") and of himself (" 'Then let me start again,' I cried /… 'I want a face that's fair this time / I want a spirit that is calm' "). Of technical interest is his use of repetition – he repeats the word "lover" seven times in the chorus. Cohen has used repetition only sparingly in his work though it appears in 'Tonight Will Be Fine' and in *The Energy Of Slaves,* one poem repeats the line "and come here and come here" all of eight times.

FIELD COMMANDER COHEN

After his visit to Israel, Cohen flew to Asmara in Ethiopia where, ensconced in the Imperial Hotel, he finished rewriting 'Chelsea Hotel number 2' and began several other songs, including this one. His military self-promotion may reflect the theatre of war he had recently known, but the theme is once again personal, and once again it reflects Cohen's dissatisfaction with the current state of his life.

There is irony rather than self-aggrandisement in the CV he presents – "our most important spy / Wounded in the line of duty / Parachuting acid into diplomatic cocktail parties". This is a metaphor for his efforts as a "worker in song", an activist in the counter-culture revolution of "sex and drugs and rock'n'roll", not an admission of espionage. His assessment of his achievement is bleak – "many men are falling where you promised to stand guard". He describes himself as "the grocer of despair working for the Yankee dollar" (more self-aware and self-deprecating humour) and, prefiguring the "twenty years of boredom" acknowledged in 'First We Take Manhattan', refers to "other forms of boredom advertised as poetry". The listener may perhaps conclude that he doth protest too much and look elsewhere for a fuller and fairer critique of his *œuvre*.

WHY DON'T YOU TRY

A plinking banjo and a gentle melodic woodwind provide the flowing accompaniment to what must be classed as a love song. But it is a curious one. The singer is begging his lover to leave him. "Why don't you try to do without him / Why don't you try to live alone... I know you're gonna make it on your own, " he sings. "Do you really need his hands for your passion? / Do you really need his heart for your throne?" he asks. Rather ungallantly anatomising their relationship, he enquires whether she needs "to hold a leash to be a lady". The single life has many more attractions – "This life is filled with many sweet companions / Many satisfying one night stands", he argues.

That it is the protagonist's own interests rather than his lover's which are his true motivation is revealed when he asks, "Do you need his labour for your baby?" One doesn't need a degree in psychology to observe that most women do wish for some assistance from the father of their child during its infancy. As the song meanders into an obscure meditation on the nursery-rhyme characters Jack and Jill, one is left with the feeling that Cohen's usually acute touch when discussing male-female relationships has deserted him here.

THERE IS A WAR

The instances of military and sociological conflict that Cohen enumerates to start and to end this song do not indicate any particular interest in the political debate or the social turmoil of the times. The 'war' that concerns him has only two combatants – Suzanne Elrod and himself. "I live here with a woman and a child, the situation makes me kind of nervous", he sings in clearly autobiographical mode (his son Adam was not yet two when the album was recorded). Suzanne, he opines, cannot stand that he is no longer "so easy to defeat... to control". An unpleasantly partisan and rather bilious little song.

A SINGER MUST DIE

There is a definite 'Kurt Weill-esque' feeling to this song, and Cohen has claimed it is "political in a certain way", but it is not easy to delineate its political content without stretching the definition of politics beyond its lexicographical snapping point. The song's narrative is not clear enough to assist us. "Is it true you betrayed us? / The answer is yes / Then read me the list of the crimes that are mine..." he sings, but pronoun usage is at best ambiguous – who asks the question? Who admits the treachery? Does "us" include or exclude the "me" character?

"Your vision is right, my vision is wrong / I'm sorry for smudging the air with my song" – does Cohen accept he is guilty of the charge that he has a "lie in his voice" or is he being ironic? Is the excuse he offers in the final verse ("Yes and long live the state by whoever it's made / Sir, I didn't see nothing, I was just getting home late") the fawning cringe of the *collaborateur* or the secretly defiant sarcasm of the *maquisard*? The matter is obviously 'void for uncertainty', as the lawyers say, and one can only conclude that a Court of Appeal would be obliged to quash his conviction for that reason alone.

I TRIED TO LEAVE YOU

A more honest take on his emotional difficulties than 'Why Don't You Try' earlier on the album, Cohen here shows us that he bears some responsibility for the relationship's survival. "I closed the book on us at least a hundred times," he sings, but inevitably "I'd wake up every morning by your side" – the singer is "a man still working for your smile". So it's not all her fault!

'I Tried To Leave You' is one of Cohen's shortest recorded songs, but in concert it became one of his most extended, as he used it as a vehicle for introducing the band.

 ### WHO BY FIRE

This song is based on the Hebrew prayer 'Mi Bamayim, Mi Ba Esh' which is sung at Yom Kippur. The reawakening of Cohen's interest in Judaism from a religious perspective was still some years away, so it is likely that the song is a response to the more politically-oriented interest in Israel which prompted his visit the previous year. It is worth noting that the war with Egypt coincided with Yom Kippur, so it is probable that Cohen would have heard it then (though he would certainly have known it from his childhood visits to the family synagogue in Montreal).

Stylistically, the song is notable for its grammatical oddity. No verb completes any of the "who by... " sequence of questions, though this is obviously deliberate. Cohen remains a professional writer whose meaning may sometimes be obscure but whose literary craftsmanship is unimpeachable.

"And who shall I say is calling?" – you do not need me to tell you that it is Death.

 ### TAKE THIS LONGING

This is a reworking of an earlier song 'The Bells', recorded by Buffy Sainte-Marie on her 1971 album *She Used To Wanna Be A Ballerina*, though there is no evidence that Cohen himself ever performed the original version. The principal difference between the two versions is the addition of the chorus line from which the later version takes its title.

There have been claims that – like 'Joan Of Arc' on his previous album – this song reflects Cohen's unrequited longing for the singer Nico. His attitude to the loved one in this song is significantly different from his attitude in those songs on this album which, from contextual evidence, we can identify as being about Suzanne Elrod. It is, however, usually a mistake to treat a song simply as biographical source material and it is reasonable both on first principles and from what we know of Cohen's life to deduce that he has felt such longing on many occasions and for many different women. Without a detailed (and pointless) analysis of which of his women friends has ever worn a "hired blue gown", it is safer to regard this song as describing the sort of universal experience which we look to the poet to describe.

 ### LEAVING GREEN SLEEVES

"Variation upon a theme of Henry Tudor" would be an apt subtitle for this song which plays with elements of 'Greensleeves', the famous sixteenth-century air allegedly written by Henry VIII himself and certainly attributable to a member of his court. There are echoes of the original melody in Cohen's song and it opens with deliberately archaic language. "Alas my love you did me wrong / To cast me out discourteously / For I have lovéd you so long / Delighting in your very company."

But whereas the royal song was written to win the favours of a fair lady, Cohen has already enjoyed those of his – "I sang my songs, I told my lies / To lie between your matchless thighs". He is at the other end of a romance. "I saw you naked in the early dawn / ... I hoped you would be someone new" he tells her, clearly earning himself a refund of his charm-school fees. So far, so similar to the themes he has developed in the album's previous songs. The difference this time is that, appropriately for the album's concluding track, both parties not only recognise that their affair has reached its terminus but are ready to disembark – "I reached for you but you were gone / So lady I'm going too". After the misery that has infused the album, one cannot see this as other than a healthy and a hopeful development.

DEATH OF A LADIES' MAN

(First issued November 1977)

The travails Cohen endured during the recording of Death Of A Ladies' Man have become legendary. At first sight, his collaboration with Phil Spector seemed a marriage made in heaven. Cohen wanted the more robust sound that Spector – begetter of the 'Wall of Sound' behind such Sixties' hits as 'Be My Baby', 'You've Lost That Lovin' Feelin' ' and 'River Deep, Mountain High' – was sure to provide. Both Cohen and Spector were Jewish; both had lost their fathers at a young age; and both (whisper it) appeared to be some way past their commercial prime. Cohen has said that he had hoped to find Debussy; in the event, he encountered Wagner.

The album was recorded in Los Angeles, Cohen having arranged a release from Columbia to enable him to record for Warner Brothers. In one sense, it was a true collaboration – Cohen provided all the lyrics and Spector all the music, even for songs Cohen had already performed live. All songs were credited to 'Spector/Cohen'. Alas, the sessions were bedevilled by the fact that neither man was in the peak of mental health. Unfortunately, their symptoms were diametrically opposed. "My flip out", Cohen tells us, "was withdrawal and melancholy and his was megalomania and insanity." Drink, drugs and guns were present in abundance. In a famous incident, "Phil approached me with a bottle of Manishewitz, kosher red wine, in one hand and a .45 in the other, put his arm around my shoulder and shoved the revolver into my neck and said 'Leonard, I love you.' " Cohen replied, with admirable sang-froid, "I hope you do, Phil."

The project ended in predictable confusion. Once Cohen had completed 'scratch tracks' (guide vocals to be replaced by definitive ones once the backing had been recorded), Spector took possession of the tapes ("he confiscated them under armed guard") and mixed the album in secret. Cohen dissociated himself from the resultant LP, calling it a "catastrophe" (though he confessed in 1985 that "I feel a lot more tender about the album now"). Nonetheless, *Death Of A Ladies' Man* undoubtedly marks the nadir of Cohen's recording career, its "wall of sound" immuring a voice more delicate and lyrics more subtle than Spector was accustomed to working with.

The album was released in November 1977 to a chorus of critical disapprobation. The cover featured a photo of Cohen and Suzanne with their friend Eva La Pierre, a Québecoise model Cohen had met on Hydra. Their photographic togetherness belied the parlous state of their relationship – Suzanne would leave him before the album had been in the shops six months – and offered a curious echo of Marianne Ihlen's photo on the cover of *Songs From A Room*, which was recorded after their break-up.

TRUE LOVE LEAVES NO TRACES

Cohen's change of musical direction in *Death Of A Ladies' Man* is graphically demonstrated in this song. Reading the lyrics (in a familiar pattern, Cohen reuses two verses from a 1961 poem 'As Mist Leaves No Scar'), one can easily imagine it as a typical 'early period' Cohen song, not out of place on *Songs Of Leonard Cohen* or *Songs From A Room*. Listening to Spector's treatment shows the distance Cohen has travelled. The syrupy backing and what can only be described as a shopping-arcade tune suggest that he is travelling involuntarily. The song has been kidnapped.

IODINE

Cohen had performed an earlier version of this song, co-written by John Lissauer on the 1975 tour and known then (for no very obvious reason) as 'Guerrero'. This version is completely rewritten. Interestingly, its opening has a Ronettes-like backing and there are hints of 'traditional Cohen' in the vocal line, though the song develops into more of a singalong as it progresses.

Thematically it is similar to many of the songs on *New Skin For The Old Ceremony*, which doubtless reflects Cohen's preoccupations when the original version was penned. Again we have a failed or failing relationship, and again it is *she* who has rejected *him*. "You let me love you till I was a failure / Your beauty on my bruise like iodine", the song's key statement, parallels the charge Cohen lays on his lover in 'There Is A War'. *Plus ça change...*

PAPER-THIN HOTEL

At last, having mined a rich seam of emotion in the colliery of failing relationships, Cohen delivers a song of acceptance, of coming to terms with loss. And, as we have come to expect, he approaches the subject from an unconventional, some might say bizarre, angle. He accepts his loss, lets go of his emotions, on hearing his lover "making love to him" through the paper-thin walls of the hotel they are both inhabiting.

The song's erotic charge is palpable, the description of their union graphically carnal. Yet, in circumstances which would drive most lovers frantic with jealousy, "I was not seized by jealousy at all"; instead, "a heavy burden lifted from my soul". It is not, of course, that the singer is extraordinarily devoid of emotion. Rather, he has moved beyond such concerns. "It's written on the walls of this hotel" he sings, and we may take the hotel not as a particularly jerry-built residence but as a metaphorical location: "You go to heaven once you've been to hell". Cohen has already touched bottom and is on his way back up.

MEMORIES

If Cohen had written the songs for *Grease*, perhaps this is how they would have sounded. "Frankie Laine was singing 'Jezebel' ", he begins over a classic Fifties rock'n'roll intro. The second verse locates the action on "the dark side of the gym", a wonderfully evocative image – teenage angst seen through a poet's binoculars.

The song is one of Cohen's most elegantly constructed. The emotional tension of the high-school hop is neatly sketched. The development of his relationship with "the tallest and the blondest girl" is simply and effectively described in the song's three verses. The use of repetition is judicious; the 'naked body' motif is shared amusingly by both the would-be seducer ("Won't you let me see your naked body?") and his target ("No, you cannot see... "). The overall effect is of an

affectionate and witty paean to teenage lust at the prom, beautifully complemented by the rock'n'roll background conjured up by Spector. That Cohen himself recognised the song as a success is suggested by its regular inclusion in his live set-list, the only one of the album's songs to be so honoured.

I LEFT A WOMAN WAITING

This is perhaps the album's most successful marrying of the diverse talents of Cohen and Spector, with its melodic flute and woodwind accompaniment and a bass line that has strong echoes of Sam Cooke's 'Bring It On Home To Me' coupled with some of Cohen's sweetest (and clearest) singing. The song's first two verses were taken from 'Poem number 27' in *The Energy Of Slaves*, but the third is new. In the original poem, the protagonist tells his "faithless wife" to go to sleep, offering no mitigation of his cruel jibe that "Whatever happened to my eyes / Happened to your beauty". In the song, they seek (and the tenor of the song suggests they find) salvation in the fervour of animal-like copulation – "Quick as dogs and truly dead we were / And free as running water". It was never the sex that gave Cohen a problem, only its emotional wake.

DON'T GO HOME WITH YOUR HARD-ON

This was another song that Cohen had performed on his 1975 tour, in a version co-written by John Lissauer. It is hard to believe that this cacophonous version is an improvement, though the raw (in every sense) material which Cohen brought to the table was hardly calculated to produce a subtle finished article. It is difficult to decipher what he is on about. The advice offered in the title is hardly of universal applicability. More sensible is the injunction against trying to "melt it down in the rain" – any man dealing with an erection in that fashion would certainly be courting legal disaster.

Bob Dylan and Allen Ginsberg were in town the night of the recording and were persuaded to add their pennyworth to the chorus. "Spector was taking a lot of cocaine," Ginsberg later remembered, "and was in a kind of hysterical frenzy, totally Hitlerian and dictatorial and sort of crazed – he started pushing us all around, saying 'get in there, get on the microphone!' – the whole thing was total chaos." 'Nuff said.

FINGERPRINTS
Ira B. Nadel has called this song "a primeval hoe-down" and that certainly describes this flippantly amusing little song, by some distance the shortest on the album. Based on another earlier poem ('Give Me Back My Fingerprints', included in *Parasites Of Heaven*), this Country & Western romp recalls Cohen's earliest performing days with The Buckskin Boys, though surely they never sang anything as bizarre as these lyrics. The song's central conceit is that Cohen's fingerprints have been wiped off while "leafing through your hair" – an obvious metaphor for loss of identity. From this runway the song takes flight, till the protagonist rejects his lover when she declares her desire to marry him, on the unusual grounds that "I can't face the dawn / With any girl who knew me / When my fingerprints were on". There is of course no obligation to marry in such circumstances.

DEATH OF A LADIES' MAN
The recording of this song demonstrates in miniature the chaotic circumstances in which the whole album was produced. The session started at 7:30 one evening. By 3:30 the next morning, with the musicians now on quadruple time, they had not yet played the song all the way through. Spector's response to this delay was at least original – he took their scores away so they could not play more than six bars at a time. At 4:00 a.m. he finally asked Cohen, who had been sitting around idly all evening, to begin singing. He did so, and the vocals were done in one take. The unsurprisingly tired and weary voice suits the song perfectly.

Much ink has been spilled anatomising the significance of the plural 'Ladies' ' in the song/album title and the singular 'Lady's' used in the book of almost the same name that Cohen published the following year. In my opinion, the singular form would have suited the song better than the plural. There is clearly only one 'she' in the narrative, and the song reprises all we have already learned about Cohen's relationship with Suzanne Elrod. The downbeat conclusion – "So the great affair is over / But whoever would have guessed / It would leave us all so vacant / And so deeply unimpressed" – was not only ungallant but also tempted commercial fate. Perhaps one does indeed "Go for nothing / If you really want to go that far".

RECENT SONGS

(First issued September 1979)

1978 was an unhappy year for Cohen. His mother died in February after a long illness. In the spring, Suzanne Elrod finally left him, decamping with their children to Paris. Paradoxically, however, this 'clearing of the decks' was to have a rejuvenating effect, both personally and artistically.

Recent Songs was recorded at A&M Studios in Los Angeles in the spring of 1979. It was produced by Henry Lewy, who was Joni Mitchell's producer and to whom Cohen's old friend had introduced him. (Cohen took co-producer credits.) His former producer John Lissauer was also involved, playing piano on 'Came So Far For Beauty' which he had co-written. The Texan band Passenger played on several tracks; a Mexican mariachi band was used on others. In honour of his mother, "who reminded me shortly before she died of the kind of music she liked", the violin of Russian-born Raffi Hakopian was extensively used, as was John Bilezikjian's oud (the oud being an eleven-stringed Middle Eastern instrument traditionally played with an eagle's feather). Jim Devlin has commented that in this album Cohen "embraced the intimate world of chamber music". It was certainly a much more successful attempt to achieve the 'Debussy feel' he had wanted, but so obviously failed to get, on *Death Of A Ladies' Man*.

The album's original working title was 'The Smokey Life', after its first completed song. Cohen struggled to find the definitive title, settling eventually for one that was not strictly accurate – three songs dated from 1975 and one (admittedly, a cover) from as far back as 1842! The album achieved modest success: *The Times* listed it as one of the Top Ten albums of the year, though this was more a critical than a commercial judgement.

THE GUESTS

Nothing more clearly indicates Cohen's change of mood than the opening track. His voice is soft and tender, the accompaniment subtle and unostentatious. Most of all, the lyrics have escaped from the narrow autobiographical rut in which he had previously seemed stuck.

The song, on which Cohen acknowledged the influence of the Persian poets Attar and Rumi for imagery, is not easy to interpret. My best guess is that the party which "the guests" attend "in every style of passion" is life itself. Some dance, some weep, but "No-one knows where the night is going / And no-one knows why the wine is flowing". What is required to mitigate life's "lonely secrecy" is love – "Oh love, I need you... now". That Cohen's habitual pessimism has not entirely abated can be seen by the inversion of "The open-hearted many / The broken-hearted few" at the start to the "Broken-hearted many / The open-hearted few" at the end.

The background vocals were arranged and sung by Jennifer Warnes, and were the beginning of a long and fruitful collaboration between the two. "The Guests" later provided the basis for, and was one of the five songs featured in, Barrie Wexler's 1983 film *I Am A Hotel*. Although Cohen initially hated it, this "pastiche of fantasy, song and dance" went on to win a Golden Rose at the 1984 International Montreux Television Festival.

HUMBLED IN LOVE

Cohen had not, of course, forgotten the pain of his break-up with Suzanne, and he was not going to miss the opportunity of using it as base metal from which to alchemise a song. 'Humbled In Love' is cut from familiar cloth, but its tone is less astringent, its attitude more adult, than previous songs stitched from the same material. Now "not even revenge can undo" the love "pledged in the passionate night". To his lover's complaint that she has been "forced to kneel in the mud" the singer responds by asking why she turns away "From the one / Who kneels there / As deeply as thee". There is great sorrow in his conclusion that "I will never hold a woman this close", but the sorrow is less angry and less self-centred than hitherto. Progress has been made.

THE WINDOW

This slow melodic waltz is one of Cohen's most beautiful songs. Its quality derives not from its lyrical fluency, though it contains some fine poetic achievements – "The thorn of the night in your bosom / The spear of the age in your side", "Oh tangle of matter and ghost" and "Climb on your tears and be silent / Like the rose on its ladder of thorns" rank alongside the best of his lyrical constructions – but rather from the generosity of spirit which the song exhibits. It is a seductive song, but the singer is not trying to get the woman addressed into bed; he is trying to get her into a state of grace, to "gentle (her) soul".

Not for the first time, Cohen employs strong religious imagery – "the cloud of unknowing", "the new Jerusalem" and "the High Holy One" are all name-checked. This time, however, there is also a recognisably religious theme running through the song. The piece ends with a prayer that would not have disgraced the Psalmist and which any poet would have been proud to pen. "Oh bless the continuous stutter / Of the word being made into flesh."

CAME SO FAR FOR BEAUTY

Like 'The Window', 'Came So Far For Beauty' counsels resignation – if not explicitly in the lyrics then certainly in its tone. The song describes the various tactics the singer has used to win his lover's heart. At first, "I practiced on my sainthood"; later "I stormed the old casino / For the money and the flesh" (wherein Cohen explicitly reprises a phrase from 'Chelsea Hotel number 2'). All to no avail. The final verse, with which the song also opens, leaves one in no doubt as to the cost the protagonist has paid for his journey – "I came so far for beauty / I left so much behind / My patience and my family / My masterpiece unsigned". But self-pity is no longer the dominant emotion (for which, much thanks).

This song, co-written by John Lissauer, was originally recorded for Cohen's abandoned 1974 album *Songs For Rebecca* and was played on his 1975 tour. Lissauer rejoined Cohen for this recording, arranging the song and playing the piano which provides the main accompaniment.

THE LOST CANADIAN (UN CANADIEN ERRANT)

'Un Canadien Errant' was written in 1842 by the celebrated French-Canadian writer Antoine Gerin-Lajoie (1824-1882). It was translated by the rather less illustrious Edith Fulton Fowke for inclusion in her collection *Chansons De Québec*. Her translation is far from adequate - the French word "errant" would be better rendered as "wandering" and her versification has all the sophistication of a greetings card. Interestingly, the film of his 1979 tour, *Song Of Leonard Cohen*, contains a scene in which Cohen plays a tape of the French section of the song and provides his own line-by-line translation. One rather wishes he had used it here.

The album's sleeve notes contain a curious historical error. The 1837 rebellion in Upper and Lower Canada was not *against* Mackenzie and Papineau, as the notes state, but was led *by* them. Since this was one of the formative events in Canadian history, it is a surprisingly basic mistake for a well-educated man to make. I guess even the best students are inattentive at the occasional lesson.

The lament of the "Canadian lad / Exiled from hearth and home" after the rebellion's bloody collapse provided an appropriate metaphor for Cohen's state of mind, though in his case it was not a homeland but a wife and family that "je ne... verrai plus".

THE TRAITOR

Another sweetly poignant song, with a heart-breakingly sad violin in the background. 'The Traitor' contains some fine writing; the choice of verb in the line "A suntanned woman *yawned* me through the summer" is wonderfully evocative.

The narrative tells a familiar story of love and loss, with particular emphasis on the narrow line dividing triumph from disaster –"The Judges said 'You missed it by a fraction' " and "I lingered on her thighs a fatal moment". Cohen is willing to accept some share of the responsibility, the 'shabby ending' being "half my fault and half the atmosphere". He accepts too his diminished and disgraced status – "So daily I renew my idle duty /... and people call me Traitor to my face". But the military metaphor employed in the fourth and sixth verses is not entirely successful. Cohen fails to establish how the 'men of action' or the 'younger soldiers' are relevant to the explicitly personal relationship the song describes.

An earlier version of this song was played on his 1975 tour, under the name 'The Traitor Song'. The sleevenotes thank Lissauer for his assistance with the earlier work, which had some major differences in the lyrics and melody, but he does not play on this version and did not receive a co-writer's credit.

OUR LADY OF SOLITUDE

This song is a longer adaptation of the poem 'All Summer Long' from Cohen's book *Death Of A Lady's Man*. At first sight, it appears to be the tender reminiscence of a summer romance, opening with the line "All summer long she touched me". In the second line, however, Cohen tells us that "she gathered in my soul". This suggests, for all the song's sensuality, that its subject is spiritual not carnal. It has more the character of a prayer than of a love song.

The Montreal in which Cohen grew up was a profoundly Catholic city, and he cannot have failed to notice Catholicism's pervasive Mariolatry. Here he creates another, new aspect of the multi-faceted Notre Dame. When we remember "Our Lady of the Harbour" from his first recorded song 'Suzanne', we can begin to see how far Leonard Cohen has travelled in the dozen or so years of his professional musical career.

Garth Hudson of The Band guested on 'Yamaha', playing alongside Passenger and the oboist Earle Dumier on this recording, though he did not join Cohen on the tour that followed, the only occasion on which the song has been given a live outing.

THE GYPSY'S WIFE

If the previous song contains lyrical echoes of his early work, then this one prefigures his most recent. The lines "These are the Final Days, this is / The Darkness, this is the Flood" echo the mood achieved a dozen or so years later in 'The Future'. There is a brooding sense of menace in this slow, melancholy song. Cohen often took years to complete a song, but this one was written with greater despatch. "My own marriage was breaking up," Cohen has said, "and in a sense it was written for *my* Gypsy wife... but in another way it's just a song about the way men and women have lost one another... and become gypsies to each other."

Garth Hudson again plays on this track, this time on accordion, along with Passenger's bassist Charles Roscoe Beck and the album's 'alternative band' Bilezikjian and Hakopian, whose mournful violin perfectly establishes the song's Romany mood.

THE SMOKEY LIFE

This song, with its "lazy, hazy, smoke-filled-bar jazz-like mood" as Jim Devlin describes it in *In Every Style Of Passion*, is the third of the album's songs to have been tried out on Cohen's 1975 tour. Then it was called 'I Guess It's Time' and co-credited to John Lissauer, though as with 'The Traitor' the album version is credited solely to Cohen.

Again, this is a song dealing with a failed or failing relationship, but there is no anger. The tone is resigned and accepting, even tender, albeit with a strong sense of weariness. Having "long ago... agreed to keep it light", the relationship is now 'light enough' for the lovers not only to "be married one more night" but also "to let it go".

What, one might ask, is "the Smokey Life (that) is practiced everywhere"? That knowing and too-clever branch of conspiracy theory that seeks out drug references in popular song will lick its lips and say "A-ha, I smell marijuana!" This, as is usually the case, is not only simplistic but unsupported by any internal evidence. The stanza which concludes with the "Smokey Life" line begins with "the scenery... fading"; next, the singer's lover learns "to walk on air"; then "the ground is gone". The answer is clear: the 'Smokey Life' is one where all solidity, all tangible reference points have evaporated. The thrust of the song is that, when this happens (as it does, "everywhere"), one must not panic. One must continue; one must survive.

BALLAD OF THE ABSENT MARE

The sleevenotes tell us that Cohen based this song on his teacher Roshi's "exposition of an ancient Chinese text". The text is question is a twelfth-century piece by the Chinese master Ka-Kuan, variously known as 'Ten Ox-Herding Pictures' or 'The Ten Bulls'. The oxen represent ten steps on the road to spiritual enlightenment.

Cohen westernises the ox-herding image, setting the song in the cowboy lands of North America. The 'prairie mood' is beautifully and authentically established by the violins, trumpets, guitars, biguela and guitarron of the accompanying mariachi band. The song's central narrative tells of a cowboy's loss of his mare, a devastating loss for one in his line of business, and his subsequent search for her, their reunion, and their final disappearance. Dorman and Rawlins see the song as "an allegory of his [Cohen's] broken romance" and it can certainly be read as such. But this is too narrow an interpretation of this richly complex "prayer for the cowboy", and ignores the clear steer Cohen provides in the sleevenotes.

A better interpretation is to see it as an allegory of desire, a meditation on the spiritual futility of carnal distractions. If there is autobiography in the song, it is not a recapitulation of Cohen's relationship with Suzanne, or with any other woman, but his pursuit of sexual pleasure and freedom, his longing "To roll and to feed / In the sweet mountain grass". When his "darling" advises him to "just let it go by", she is not recommending forgiveness of a lover's unkindness, as Cohen was when he used the same phrase in 'Bird On The Wire'. She is counselling the abandonment of desire. The final lines accept the challenge: "So I pick out a tune / And they [cowboy and mare] move right along / And they're gone like the smoke / And they're gone like this song." We have come a long way from the bleak ending of 'Death Of A Ladies' Man' which concluded Cohen's previous album.

VARIOUS POSITIONS

(First issued February 1985)

If *Recent Songs* represents site-clearance, *Various Positions* can be seen as the first storey of a new building. In the five or six years between the two albums, Cohen had experienced that "certain moment when you have to look into the face of your own activity and discern exactly what you're doing and who you are". He has said that, until he came to record *Various Positions*, he "had no idea how hard the task [of writing songs] was", though it is clear from the quote's context that he is talking less about writing *per se* than about writing well. "I began to apply myself with a very special dedication to this dismal activity called songwriting," Cohen commented regarding this period of his life.

Although the turmoil of his relationship with Suzanne Elrod was now history and he had established a new relationship with Dominique Issermann, Cohen had other problems. He was reportedly broke, and he felt his career had more or less evaporated. Nonetheless, the darkest hour being just before dawn, he was beginning to gain the critical acclaim of a new generation. Newly emerging alternative musicians like The Sisters Of Mercy and Nick Cave had discovered his music, and were performing cover versions. The position Cohen found himself in is beautifully encapsulated in the quote he attributed to CBS President Walter Yetnikoff: "Leonard, we know you're great, but we don't know if you're any good".

Various Positions was recorded in 1984 at the Quadrasonic Sound Studios in New York, and was produced by his old colleague John Lissauer. It achieved Top Ten success in Spain, Portugal and Scandinavia and more modest success in the UK. To Cohen's chagrin, Columbia decided not to release it in the USA. Although it was eventually released there, by Passport Records, only a few thousand copies were printed and, predictably, commercial success did not ensue. "A prophet is not without honour, save in his own country."

DANCE ME TO THE END OF LOVE

From the verbal felicity of its poetry ("Show me slowly what I only know the limits of") to the private sensuality of its sentiments ("Let me see your beauty when the witnesses are gone"), this tender hymn to carnal love marks the beginning of a new and more mature phase in Cohen's songwriting. Set to an up-tempo dance rhythm, with Jennifer Warnes providing back-up vocals, the song seems at first sight a simple one.

Further reflection reveals its complexity. If it exhibits the joy of newly-established love, and there is a patent sense of contentment that Cohen had rarely shown before, it is no piece of bliss-addled naivety. Cohen has learnt from, but does not eschew, his experience. The 'end of love' to which he proposes to dance suggests he has no young man's illusion that love will last forever. But the word "end" implies not only finality but also, and here we see the experienced poet at work, purpose. Nor has he forgotten his old friend, existential fear. "Dance me through the panic till I'm gathered safely in" he asks his lover, seeking "a tent of shelter" in their shared embrace.

Something of the importance of this song in the Cohen catalogue can be gauged from its having been his usual concert opener ever since he recorded it. It was also chosen as the album's single. For the first time, Cohen produced a promotional video, shot in black and white and set in a hospital. That it was directed by Dominique Issermann neatly closed the loop linking Cohen's personal and professional development.

COMING BACK TO YOU

In tone, this song continues in the mature if in this case resigned mood heard in 'Dance Me To The End Of Love'. The slow, countrified ballad style contrasts with and complements the previous song. But the obvious question which the song raises – coming back to whom? – poses a problem for the thesis that Cohen's songwriting has become new and more mature. If Cohen is still harking back to a previous relationship, perhaps to Suzanne Elrod, has he really progressed that much?

Unlike those of his songs sparked from the embers of dying love, however, the mood here is much more reflective and the writing much less obviously autobiographical. There is much less of a sense of an ex-lover's personality than infuses earlier songs; the emotion seems much more generic, as if the song is a distillation of the experience of loss rather than the depiction of one particular loss. Perhaps it is love itself, rather than a specific woman, to whom Cohen is returning.

It is also possible that the song's subject is not human love at all, but art. The art of writing was not only a subject in which Cohen had long been interested, but was also something he was thinking a great deal about when he wrote this song. It is therefore a very plausible reading of the song that what he is 'coming back to' is, to speak poetically, his Muse. If that is so, then the song is persuasive evidence that the Muse has indeed answered his call.

THE LAW

Despite its references to the Law, to guilt and to angels, this is not in fact a religious song. 'Law' may be a direct translation of the word 'Torah', which Jews use to describe the first five books of the Bible, but the phrase "I fell with my angel" contradicts the Hasidic principle that angels can neither deteriorate nor improve. Guilt may be a pervasive Catholic emotion, and thus familiar to Cohen from his upbringing in Montreal, but the suggestion that "You just don't ask for mercy / While you're still on the stand" is distinctly at odds with Catholic theology and practice.

Cohen has said of this song that "it's got something to do with the fact that there are consequences to our activities", a point echoed by Bruce Springsteen's comment that we live, and that songwriters must therefore write about, "a life with consequences". This idea may contain spiritual wisdom, but it is more a humanist than a religious message. It is also a message consonant with the spiritual and artistic progress that Cohen exhibits throughout *Various Positions*. We can also see Cohen taking a 'position' here that runs against fashionable contemporary thinking. As he put it, "even though we are living in an age when guilt is… regarded as a disease, it is still the only way that we know we've made a mistake".

NIGHT COMES ON

Ira B. Nadel has called this "one of the most troubling songs on the album, and perhaps the most autobiographical". The song certainly contains what seem to be autobiographical elements. The singer's mother appears in the first verse, his father (who had been wounded during the First World War) in the second, his children in the third; the reference in verse 5 to "Bill's Bar" sounds realistic too. But the song is not reportage, and none of the actions ascribed to the mother, father or children identify them individually. Indeed, the song's literal suggestion that Cohen's father fought alongside him in Egypt is patently false. In terms of the song's structure and development, his mother, father and children are more symbolic characters than flesh-and-blood ones.

The song is troubling, however, in the sense that it is both difficult and bleak. His mother, who lies "under the marble and the snow", is offering her advice from beyond the grave. "Go back to the World" she tells him, suggesting that the "night" he wants "to go on and on" is death itself – a suggestion reinforced in the song's final lines where he sings "I want to cross over, I want to go home".

The sense of despair is enhanced by some elegant writing, from the typically Cohenesque paradox "I needed so much / To have nothing to touch / I've always been greedy that way" to the disillusioned toast, "Here's to the few / Who forgive what you do / And the fewer who don't even care". Of course, emotional bleakness and personal despair are hardly new territory for Cohen. What is different here, and what redeems both the singer and the song, is the knowledge that he must follow his mother's command and "Go back to the World", the world where, in a felicitous phrase, his children 'hide'.

HALLELUJAH

On hearing *Various Positions*, Bob Dylan commented that Cohen's songs were becoming more like prayers, and 'Hallelujah' certainly falls into that category. Its biblical references and the apparently religious denouement ("I'll stand before the Lord of Song / With nothing on my tongue but Hallelujah") give it a psalm-like quality. But this is no simply religious song. As so often when Cohen uses religious imagery, secular themes intrude. In the second verse, it is the domesticating force of the beautiful woman that compels "the baffled king" into song. The fourth and final verse, with its confession that "I couldn't feel so I tried to touch", seems as much about Cohen's relationship with his sexuality as about his relationship with God.

Nonetheless, it is a powerful and moving song. Maybe it does not matter whether one hears "the holy or the broken Hallelujah". The rhymes for 'Hallelujah' are skilfully chosen, surprising yet not detracting from the sense. The subject of the pronoun 'you' is open to question (it clearly refers to David in the second verse, but less obviously so in the first and third), but such imprecision is found often enough in Cohen's work to suggest it is intended.

It is known that Cohen spent a long time writing the song, and he has revised it several times since. There is an amusing story that, having been asked by Dylan how long it took him to write the song, Cohen (by his own admission) lied and said it took "three or four years", when in fact it had taken longer. Reciprocating with the same question about Dylan's 'I And I', Cohen was told it had taken fifteen minutes. His later comment that "I believed him" was, it need hardly be said, not made under oath.

'Hallelujah' has been extensively covered by other artists, with notable versions by John Cale, Jeff Buckley (a posthumous American number one) and Rufus Wainwright. In addition, British singer Alexandra Burke rose to fame after winning the fifth series of UK TV series *The X Factor* in 2008 with a rather histrionic reading of the song that, when released as a single, became the current European record holder for single sales over a period of 24 hours, selling 105,000 copies in one day. It was also the top-selling song of the year in the UK, and became the 2008 UK Christmas number one single. By January 2009, UK sales of Burke's version of 'Hallelujah' had passed one million copies, a first for a British female soloist.

THE CAPTAIN

From the psalmodic mood of 'Hallelujah', Cohen changes tack abruptly and offers a countrified toe-tapping ballad. With its honky-tonk piano and hoe-down fiddle, and its worldly and cynical lyrics, this dialogue between a dying Captain and the soldier to whom he is bequeathing his command seems at first sight a simple piece of narrative fun. But given its musical context, the soldier's statement that "I risked my life, but not to hear / Some country-western song" gives us a clue that Cohen is being far from simple here.

The story the song tells is overtly one about inheritance. In 'The Night Comes On' two songs earlier, the singer's father instructs him to "Try to go on / Take my books, take my gun / And remember, my son, how they lied". 'The Captain' is a more extended meditation on that theme. So what is the inheritance in question?

One reading is that it is the Jewish tradition. "Complain, complain, that's all you've done / Ever since we lost, / If it's not the Crucifixion / Then it's the Holocaust", the Captain upbraids the soldier, echoing many a Jewish joke and reflecting an anti-Semitism both ancient and modern. Lines like "There is no decent place to stand / In a massacre" and "I'm on the side that's always lost" seem to bear this out. But this is a song, so we need not restrict ourselves to a single interpretation. The song can also, and simultaneously, be seen as describing the handing on of an artistic baton, perhaps one carved in the literary circles Cohen frequented in his youth. One may also ask,

given that Cohen was in his fifties when he wrote the song, whether he identifies himself with the testator or the heir, with the dying Captain or his truculent successor. Or do both characters reflect different aspects of their creator?

In any event, the song is clearly not the simple ditty it first appears to be.

HUNTER'S LULLABY

'Hunter's Lullaby', a rare song in the Cohen catalogue in that the title appears nowhere in the lyrics, is another seemingly simple song that reveals its complexity on further examination. At first sight, it seems to be merely a re-working of an old folk song. But as the song develops, the lyrics start to deviate from the traditional story. It is clearly neither food nor fur for which the hunter has "gone a-hunting". He has gone "where only greed can enter". What, then, is he hunting?

Some commentators have seen the song as a metaphor for Cohen's career, for the search for fame and fortune ("the silver and the glass") at the expense of domestic responsibility. This is certainly a possible reading, though nothing in Cohen's career suggests that mass popular acclaim was his chief motivation. Equally, one can read the song as describing a more general 'hunting' for worldly pleasure or for freedom (perhaps especially sexual freedom). This makes more sense of the statement that "A woman cannot follow him / Although she knows the way". In this reading, the domestic scene of the mother and child left behind becomes itself a metaphor for the life of the spirit, necessarily abandoned when the carnal hunt is on.

Although there is nothing explicit in the lyrics which identifies the singer's gender, the context certainly suggests that it is sung by the wife-and-mother whom the hunter leaves behind. If so, Cohen deserves credit for not only for abandoning the tyranny of the autobiographical "I" but also for 'singing as a woman' when the song so requires. It is a mark of the serious artist that they are willing to do so – compare Bob Dylan's version of 'House Of The Rising Sun', where his adoption of a woman's persona is essential to the song's meaning, with The Animals' version, where the transcription to a male perspective renders the subject matter incomprehensible.

HEART WITH NO COMPANION

Sometimes thought of as a lightweight song, 'Heart With No Companion' may lack some of the intellectual complexity of other songs, but it is a beautiful song in its own right and a profound expression of Cohen's Buddhist beliefs. Compassion lies at the heart of Buddhism, and the song distills the essence of compassion, applying it to various cases of suffering or loss evoked with all Cohen's typical linguistic inventiveness. (Note too that, as so often in Cohen's work, for all its spiritual theme, the lyric employs no overtly religious language.)

Cohen's compassion derives not only from his Buddhism, but also from personal experience. "I greet you from the other side / Of sorrow and despair" he opens the song, repeating the verse at its end. But whereas he might once have turned his 'sorrow and despair' into mournful self-pity or the character assassination of an ex-lover, he has now refined it into "A love so vast and shattered / It will reach you everywhere". He has trod the path of suffering and reached the garden of wisdom.

IF IT BE YOUR WILL

The album ends with the most overtly religious song that Cohen has ever written. Based, both lyrically and musically, on a synagogue prayer ("May it therefore be Your will, Lord our God") recited on the eve of Yom Kippur, the Jewish Day of Atonement, 'If It Be Your Will' is (unusually for Cohen) equally religious in sentiment and in language. It is a prayer expressing total surrender to the divine will.

The song offers an interesting counterpoint to 'Heart With No Companion' which precedes it. That song focuses on the individual's relationship with the human race, this one on the individual's relationship with God. It is also much more monotheistic in tone, and consequently less Buddhist in its theology. This may be an example of Cohen taking 'various positions', though if it is read as referring to his Zen master Joshi's will, the contradiction is resolved.

Cohen's own comments on 'If It Be Your Will' indicate its importance in the personal and professional development that is evident throughout *Various Positions*. Cohen admitted that the song "took a long time to write because the lyric and the melody are so simple that if there were a false step it would really collapse the structure; it would dissolve and be left hanging... But I think it's probably one of the best songs I've ever written."

I'M YOUR MAN

(First issued February 1988)

I'm Your Man was recorded in Los Angeles, Montreal and Paris, with assistance from various former colleagues such as Jennifer Warnes, Roscoe Beck, John Bilezikjian and Raffi Hakopian. The album was mostly self-produced, although Michel Robidoux received a co-production credit for 'Everybody Knows' and 'I'm Your Man' and Jean-Michel Reusser one for 'Take This Waltz'.

Cohen made an important change to his songwriting technique for I'm Your Man. Previously he had used a guitar when writing and had been, as he modestly put it, "limited by my facility on guitar". This time, he used a synthesiser and found a far greater range of rhythmic patterns and musical options available to him. Nevertheless, the recording of the album proved a difficult and depressing experience. Although he had spent almost two years writing the songs, he found that they did not work in the studio. "I couldn't get behind the lyrics... I couldn't find a voice for them. So I had to start over almost every song."

That he did so, and to great effect, is reflected not just in his own judgement ("it's the most cohesive album I've ever done... it's strong, it's got eight good dogs pulling this record, there's no filler material") but also in the commercial verdict of the marketplace. *I'm Your Man* topped the charts in the UK, Norway and Spain, earned a gold disc in Canada, and was nominated 'album of the year' in both the UK and the USA. It also helped Cohen to a new self-awareness. "Now I know what I am," he announced. "I'm not a novelist. I'm not the light of my generation. I'm not the spokesman for a new sensibility. I'm a songwriter living in LA and this is my record."

One curious development marked the appearance of *I'm Your Man*. Cohen's voice had noticeably deepened since *Various Positions* three years earlier. He has attributed this to "50,000 cigarettes and a lot of booze". It is unclear whether the 50,000 cigarettes represent a lifetime figure (not a very impressive total for a lifelong smoker in his Fifties) or the number he had smoked since recording *Various Positions*, a much more self-sacrificingly heroic achievement.

 FIRST WE TAKE MANHATTAN
The opening bars of the opening track, funky and synthesised, announce immediately that *I'm Your Man* is a different sort of Cohen record to any that had gone before. When he growls into the opening phrase – "They sentenced me to twenty years of boredom" – the change of attitude is obvious. This is no reflective, spiritually enriched, philosophical offering. This is a worldly-wise, cynical, even at times angry Leonard Cohen at work: "Remember me, I used to live for music".

He has called this song "the voice of enlightened bitterness" and "a demented manifesto", and the song certainly reflects contemporary social and political images and ideas. But it is not a political song. It neither identifies the causes of problems nor proposes solutions to them. The two towns mentioned in the song offer a clue as to its real meaning. Manhattan is the nerve-centre of the music industry, and Berlin is the city Cohen has stated he finds the hardest to play. The song is really a girding-of-the-loins for the rigours of his forthcoming tour, a call-to-arms directed at his band.

The song became so popular in Athens that cool Greek dudes of the day took to greeting one another with the song's punchline. "First we take Manhattan", one would say; the reply "Then we take Berlin" identified the other as suitably hip to warrant further conversation.

 ### AIN'T NO CURE FOR LOVE

The first version of this song appeared on Jennifer Warnes' 1984 collection of Cohen songs, *Famous Blue Raincoat*. The song arose from a conversation she and Cohen had about AIDS, which at that time was beginning to emerge as a subject of public concern and debate. "This is horrible," Warnes declared, "what are people going to do? They won't stop loving each other." "Well, honey, there ain't no cure for love", Cohen replied. At Warnes' suggestion, he worked up this off-the-cuff phrase into a song.

The version on *I'm Your Man*, while recognisably the same song, differs significantly from the earlier version. The chorus and the last two verses have been rewritten, the final verse – which begins "I walked into this empty church / There was nowhere else to go" – adding religious overtones to the carnality of the opening verses. However, as so often when Cohen uses overtly religious language, the song is not offering a specifically religious message.

'Ain't No Cure For Love' was released as a single. Recent publicity about payola and corruption in the record industry, particularly in the plugging of potential hits, prompted Cohen to a satirical gesture. He sent two dollars to the CBS sales reps who would be promoting the song. There is no evidence that they were unduly influenced by the bribe.

 ### EVERYBODY KNOWS

Co-written by Cohen and Sharon Robinson, one of the backing singers on his 1979-80 tour, 'Everybody Knows' is a song of bitter-sweet cynicism, Cohen's deeper-than-ever voice providing the vinegar sweetened by Jennifer Warnes' backing vocals and John Bilezikjian's oud. Through a long list of what 'everybody knows', Cohen paints a bleak portrait of society ("Old Black Joe's still picking cotton for your ribbons and bows") and of his love-life ("There were so many people you just had to meet without your clothes").

Yet for all the undisguised despair, the song is oddly comforting. Instead of just eloquently charting his own misery, as he might have done in the past, Cohen flatters his audience by assuming that they share his hard-won insight. "Everybody knows", he sings, explicitly including his audience and implicitly excluding those who do not accept 'our' point of view. Instead of simply reporting back to us, he co-opts us into his circle of initiates: "We know this even if others don't" is the suggestion.

The song is also noteworthy as marking the first occasion Cohen played keyboards on record, a reflection no doubt of his new method of songwriting.

 ### I'M YOUR MAN

The album's title track is a hymn of seduction, suffused with all the urgency of unrequited love. All Cohen's usual verbal fluency is called into play. He offers to be, among other things, a boxer, a doctor and a driver, chat-up lines not usually found on the lips of the average love-struck swain.

What adds dimension to the song, however, is its middle section. "I've been running through these promises to you that I made and I could not keep", he sings. We can now see that the promises in the two preceding verses were not merely elegant attempts at seduction, but the promises he once made to a lover who has since left him. Perhaps they are the very promises he could not keep. No longer hopeful in the grip of love's first flowering, he is the desolate lover for whom "the beast won't go to sleep". He knows the futility of continuing his pursuit ("A man never got a woman back, not by begging on his knees") but he cannot abandon it.

It is from this standpoint that he sings the final verse. It is much more tender, even romantic, than his earlier promises, with their vainglorious declarations and erotic suggestions. These last promises are more practical and more personal and, in the achingly eloquent final line, more attuned to her needs than to his own: "If you want a father for your child, / Or only want to walk with me a while across the sand, / I'm your man".

TAKE THIS WALTZ

Cohen had first encountered the work of the Spanish poet Federico García Lorca at the age of fifteen. In literary terms, it was love at first sight. Lorca, Cohen has joked, ruined his life by leading him "into the racket of poetry". He has also said that Lorca "taught me to understand the dignity of sorrow". So profound an influence was he that Cohen even named his daughter after him, though it should be noted that Lorca has had little stylistic influence on Cohen's own poetry or songwriting, however much of an intellectual and emotional influence he has been.

'Take This Waltz' is Cohen's translation of Lorca's poem 'Pequeño Vals Vienès' from his collection *Poetas en Nueva York*. Cohen's song, which takes some liberties with the structure of Lorca's poem but is otherwise faithful to its mood and surreal imagery, was written for a tribute album compiled to honour the fiftieth anniversary of Lorca's murder by Franco's fascist soldiers in 1936. The version included on *I'm Your Man* is a remix of the 1986 version, adding Raffi Hakopian's violin and backing vocals from Jennifer Warnes.

JAZZ POLICE

If 'Take This Waltz' represents Cohen's rendition of Lorca's surrealism, then 'Jazz Police' offers some surrealism of his very own. Co-written by Jeff Fisher, a fellow Canadian who had arranged 'First We Take Manhattan', the song was inspired by events in the studio. The band were always trying to infiltrate augmented fifths and sevenths into their playing; Cohen would object, not wanting that jazzy sort of sound on his songs (though he had no objection to jazz *per se*). Teased for being a 'Jazz Policeman', he decided to turn the band's banter into a song.

The song itself betrays little of its origins. It is Cohen himself who seems to be the target for the forces of jazz law and order, though it is not at all clear what is going on in the song. It certainly contains some disturbing, not to say fascistic, ideas. Cohen has stated that he wanted to "start with very serious propositions, against racism, against, oppression, against repression, and disintegrate into meaninglessness, but with a smile." Cohen himself grew to dislike the song's conceit, but kept it on the album because its "fragmented absurdity" caught the mood of the period. In these terms, the song may be considered a success, if perhaps a success little worth achieving

I CAN'T FORGET

Following a song that began in a spirit of jeu d'esprit, 'I Can't Forget' could not have begun its life more seriously. Originally entitled 'Taken Out Of Egypt', it dealt with no less a subject than the Jewish Exodus, which Cohen intended to treat as "a metaphor for the journey of the soul from bondage into freedom". The song took months to write. Alas, when Cohen came to record it he 'cracked', finding himself unable to sing it as written. Whether he found the subject too highfalutin' or whether he felt too personally burdened to sing about release from slavery, Cohen realised he had to recast the song.

Knowing he had a good melody on his hands, he rewrote the lyrics with a much less cataclysmic and more personal theme. The song became a slightly wistful, often humorous, self-mocking portrait of the poet as an old man. Stumbling out of bed, smoking a cigarette, pulling his stomach in, preparing himself for the struggle ahead, he feels "This can't be me, must be my double". He is acting from instinct, driving a "rig that runs on memory". He has so much history; he "can't forget", but when it comes to the crunch, he can only recycle an old joke and claim "but I don't remember what".

Although it is wistful, "I Can't Forget' is far from despairing. Winter may be, in a felicitous phrase, "tuning up", but "a lot goes on forever". The love he has had all his life he intends to keep alive till the end. He is ageing, but he is not ready to be buried yet. And in his defiance, Cohen has created what must be the best serious song to have been constructed around what is essentially a rather trivial play on words.

TOWER OF SONG

'Tower Of Song' is a masterpiece. Cohen himself has called it "one of the three or four real songs that I've ever written". From the opening synthesiser riff, simple and stunning at the same time, through a set of lyrics as controlled and purposeful as any he has produced, to the sugar-sweet "dee-doo-dum-dums" as it fades, 'Tower Of Song' is a brilliantly evoked essay on the art of songwriting. With this song, Cohen has surely earned the rent-free lease of a room therein.

Like 'I Can't Forget' before it, this song had a troubled genesis. It too began life under another title, 'Raise My Voice In Song'. Oddly enough, it started out concerned with the same theme used to replace the original one in 'I Can't Forget', the problems of being an ageing singer. Cohen had abandoned the song, but this time he did not abandon the theme, and returned to the song later in Montreal.

Having finished the lyrics, he sent for an engineer and recorded it in one take, accompanying himself on a toy synthesiser. Jennifer Warnes later added the "dee-doo-dum-dums" and a few minor repairs were made, but in essence the version here is the original two-track take. One may marvel that one of Cohen's finest songs took so little effort to record, but one should remember (pace Whistler) that the experience of a lifetime is a necessary ingredient at the moment of creation.

LEONARD COHEN
THE MUSIC AND THE MYSTIQUE

1970

Cohen tours for the first time, with dates in the United States, Canada and Europe, a highlight being his appearance before over 500,000 fans at the Isle of Wight Festival in the UK.

1934

Leonard Cohen born September 21 in Montreal. As a teenager he learns to play guitar and becomes fascinated by the poetry of Federico Garcia Lorca.

1956

Starts at Columbia University. *Let Us Compare Mythologies* published.

1971

Songs Of Love And Hate
released.

1972

Son Adam born.

The Energy Of Slaves published.

1974

Daughter Lorca born.

New Skin For The Old Ceremony released.

1977

Death Of A Ladies' Man, produced
by Phil Spector, released.

1978

Death Of A Lady's Man published.

1979

Recent Songs released.

1984

Book Of Mercy published.

Various Positions
released.

1988

I'm Your Man released.

1991

Cohen is made an
Officer of the Order
of Canada.

1992

The Future released.

1994

Moves into the Mount
Baldy Zen Center in
California to begin five
years of seclusion.

1999

Leaves Mount Baldy.

2001

Ten New Songs
released.

2003

Cohen is made a Companion to the
Order of Canada, the country's
highest civilian honour recognizing a
lifetime of outstanding achievement,
dedication to the community and
service to the nation.

2008

World Tour, his first in 15 years, begins. His performance at the Glastonbury Festival in June is acclaimed by many as the highlight of the event.

A version of 'Hallelujah' by Alexandra Burke tops the UK singles chart, becoming the fastest-selling single by a female artist in UK chart history. So much interest in the song is generated that Jeff Buckley's rendition occupies the number two spot while Cohen's original version enters the singles chart at 34, his first-ever British Top 40 single. With versions of the song holding down three Top 40 UK Singles Chart positions simultaneously, 'Hallelujah' became the fastest-selling digital single in European history.

2009

On 18 September Cohen collapses on stage at a concert in Valencia, Spain, halfway through performing 'Bird On The Wire'. He is admitted to local hospital with stomach problems, and possibly food poisoning. Three days later, on his 75th birthday, he performs in Barcelona, his last in Europe in 2009 and rumoured to be his last European concert ever.

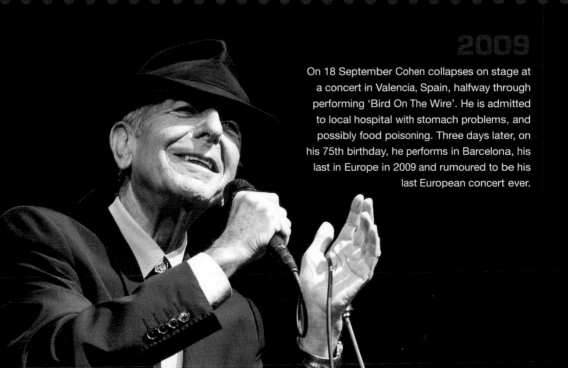

2010

World Tour ends
after 246 shows in
Europe, Australia,
Israel, Canada
and the US.

THE FUTURE

(First issued November 1992)

The Future was recorded in Los Angeles in 1992. Its original working title was *Busted*, though *Be For Real* (one of two cover songs on the album) was also considered before the final decision went in favour of *The Future*. Several of the musicians from his 1988 tour band contributed, and the album again benefits from Jennifer Warnes' backing vocals. The production credits are liberally distributed, Steve Lindsey, Bill Ginn, Leanne Ungar, Yoav Goren and Rebecca de Mornay (his latest flame) sharing the honours with Cohen himself.

The Future is an odd album in that it manages to be funny and gloomy at the same time. Neither trait was new: contrary to public misconception, Cohen has often incorporated humour in his work, albeit a wry and dark-edged humour. Gloom had been an even more frequent flavour. Here, however, it is society rather than his personal situation that depresses the artist. Some of this may be due to his residence in Los Angeles, well described by Ira B. Nadel as a "geologically and politically unstable" place. Certainly the 1992 riots, which destroyed several stores that Cohen patronised, will not have helped his mood. Cohen himself, however, has cited the collapse of the Berlin Wall in 1989 as occasioning much of the album. On this subject, Cohen took an unorthodox view. "Though it is impossible not to rejoice with those who are rejoicing," he said, "I alone among my friends produced a more gloomy prediction". He did not share the common optimism that democracy was about to flourish in the newly-liberated East.

Although, once again, many songs proved troublesome when he came to record them, and needed rewriting in the studio, *The Future* confirmed Cohen's commercial reputation. It went platinum in Canada within months of its release. In 1993, it won Cohen a Juno Award for Best Male Vocalist, and the following year 'Closing Time' won another for Best Rock Video. The new, deep voice that had been heard on *I'm Your Man* was still in evidence on *The Future*, despite Cohen having given up smoking in 1990. If anything, it was even deeper. This, combined with the dark humour, the skilful lyrics and a more mainstream-rock musicality, cast Cohen in an avuncular role – the old survivor of ancient philosophical wars returned to offer wise, witty and critical opinions on contemporary society to the young "nieces and nephews" in his audience. After thirty years, Leonard Cohen was cooler than he had ever been.

 THE FUTURE

"I've seen the future, brother, it is murder". Reading like a post-modern rendition of the New Testament Book Of Revelation, the title track offers a bleak précis of the modern world's ills. Cohen exhorts us to "REPENT" with all the vigour of an Old Testament prophet (he is, after all, "the little Jew who wrote the Bible"). Amid the collapse of civilisation as we know it, he yearns for the terrible old certainties – the Berlin Wall, Stalin, St Paul, Christ, Hiroshima. There is only one plant poking through this desolate landscape, a plant in which Cohen has shown a keen botanical interest throughout his life: "love's the only engine of survival".

The song's apocalyptic bleakness is mitigated by its up-tempo backing. "I don't think you can divorce the fact", Cohen has said, "that it's a hot little track and you can dance [to it]; if you couldn't, I think it would be really dismal... If I had just nailed that lyric to a church door like Martin Luther it would be a very grim manifesto." Cohen has in fact pulled off rather a neat trick – he has made existential despair entertaining. (And when one considers his stylistically very different early work, one might conclude that *plus ça change, plus c'est la même chose*.)

WAITING FOR THE MIRACLE

A similar sense of desolation infuses 'Waiting For The Miracle', but this time it is personal. Both the music and the lyrics are gentler than in 'The Future'; there is no "crack and anal sex" on offer here. The waiting Cohen describes has been a life-long pursuit – "I waited half my life away". He has refused invitations, spurned love, while waiting Godot-like for a miracle. It has not come yet, but after all this time Cohen is not going to give up hope now. When "they ask you how you're feeling / Of course you say you can't complain... You just say you're out there waiting / For the miracle to come".

'Waiting For The Miracle' was co-written with Sharon Robinson, with whom Cohen had collaborated on 'Everybody Knows'. Work on the song had started in the early Eighties, and versions were apparently ready for inclusion on both *Various Positions* and *I'm Your Man*. It is believed that Jennifer Warnes sang the song in concert during her 1987 tour. But in mood, and for its contrast yet continuity with the themes explored in 'The Future', it is surely in its rightful place here.

BE FOR REAL

Cohen's first cover version since 'Un Canadien Errant' on *Recent Songs*, 'Be For Real' was written by Frederick Knight, the 'Mr Knight' whom Cohen thanks at the end of the song. Cohen sings it in his gravelliest voice, the "babys" in particular seeming to hit a lower register than ever before. Nonetheless, it does seem to be something of a filler track. It is a much slighter song lyrically than any of Cohen's own, though he does sing some lyrics which do not appear in the version printed on the sleeve, suggesting that they are his own additions.

While the tone of worldly-wise and wary melancholy is not out of kilter with Cohen's own temperament, the song's dramatic situation – the beloved returning while the lover doubts the permanence of her return – is not one that Cohen himself had previously chosen to explore, though he has explored most aspects of love's failure in his time. Maybe he simply liked the song and enjoyed singing it (which is as good a reason as any for including it).

CLOSING TIME

Cohen had already recorded a version of this song, which he had taken two years to write, when he came to "the painful decision that I hadn't written it yet". He dumped the track and began again.

The final version is a four-square country stomp with a hoe-down feel. The overt scenario is end-of-evening in a crowded bar. The bar-room mood is well caught – the "Johnny Walker wisdom" is flowing and his "very sweet companion" is "rubbing half the world against her thigh". The scene is familiar to every late-night drinker the world over. There is "hell to pay when the fiddler stops" but, and one would expect no less from as accomplished as poet as Cohen, this is no mere hymn to drinking.

The mood of the song reflects not just the end of one particular evening. There is a strong sense of fin-de-siècle, of a whole era, maybe even history itself, coming to an end. In this tavern, all the customers share the bleak view of the future expressed in the album's title song. "The place" – which we may take to mean the world, or at least western civilisation – has been "wrecked / By the winds of change and the weeds of sex". It "Looks like freedom but it feels like death / It's something in between I guess".

Yet, despite the collapse of everything around him, Cohen still clings to "the only engine of survival" – "I loved you when our love was blessed / I love you now there's nothing left". Unillusioned but defiant, cynical but wise, he can still "lift his glass to the Awful Truth / Which you can't reveal to the Ears of Youth / Except to say it isn't worth a dime". 'Closing Time' is a fine song, and one worth its place on the several CD-singles it has graced.

ANTHEM

Cohen regards 'Anthem' as "one of the best songs I've written, maybe the best". It was certainly one of the most difficult to get right. He had begun it in 1982 under the title 'Ring The Bells', and had recorded versions of it during the sessions for both *Various Positions* and *I'm Your Man*. But on both occasions "there was a lie somewhere in there... a disclosure that I was refusing to make... a solemnity that I hadn't achieved". This time, with Rebecca de Mornay's help, he nailed it.

The song's theme is survival – personal, spiritual and emotional – in an imperfect world. Wars will be re-fought. The dove of peace is ever in bondage. The sum of the parts does not equal the whole. Again, love is the key, but it comes "like a refugee". The centrepiece of the song is its chorus. "Ring the bells that still can ring", the singer announces, finding music amid the debris. "Forget your perfect offering", he counsels, for perfection cannot be achieved in this imperfect world. Hence the observation, "There is a crack in everything", before the punchline that makes his point: "That's how the light gets in".

Some commentators have noted the song's borrowings from cabbalistic sources, in particular from the sixteenth-century rabbi Isaac Luria. It is also worth noting a possible borrowing from Native American culture, according to which shamans derived their power from having a cracked skull through which supernatural powers denied to the whole-skulled majority could enter.

DEMOCRACY

As with several songs on the album, Cohen had difficulty writing 'Democracy', but it was a problem of a different order to the one he had faced with 'Closing Time'. On this occasion, the problem was selecting from the eighty-odd verses he had written. (On his 1993 tour, he sometimes introduced the song by reciting some of the discarded verses.)

In keeping with the album's theme, and its title, 'Democracy' presents another view of the future. This time, Cohen takes a hopeful stance. Despite its social, sexual, racial and emotional problems, there is hope for the United States of America – democracy is coming.

This rare excursion of Cohen's into political territory derives from two ideas. The first is his belief, contradicting many pundits' comments, that democracy was unlikely to take root in the Eastern European countries whose Communist regimes were collapsing as he wrote. He did not see "a territory that has produced everybody from Dracula to Ivan the Terrible to Stalin" as a fertile breeding ground for democratic politics. One can recognise the ancestral memories of his mother's Russian forebears even if one must – at the time of writing – suspend judgement on his historical prediction.

The second idea behind the song is that the USA has not yet achieved democracy. Superficially, this is obviously untrue. In the sense of democracy as the genuine operation of body politic by and for the people, it is easier to agree that present-day American political structures leave much to be desired. As a foreign national in the USA, Cohen is a candid friend, making the neat distinction "I love the country but I can't stand the scene", and describing America even-handedly as "the cradle of the best and of the worst". In writing what amounts to a prayer for political improvement, one can imagine Cohen metaphorically revisiting the summer camp of his youth where he and his friends had sung their way through *The People's Songbook*.

LIGHT AS THE BREEZE

A sense of carnality permeates this song, though I think it is too narrow a construction to see it, as Devlin has, as "an erotic narrative… detailing the act of cunnilingus". It is true that the singer kneels "at the delta", a clear reference to the female pudenda, but the structure of the song indicates that, while Cohen is talking about more than just holding hands, his subject is wider than one specific act.

The six verses are separated into three pairs by the song's chorus. The singer's attitude to carnal love develops, and the act of kneeling takes on a different significance, in each pair of verses. In the first pair, we can see a young man's wonder and delight at the act of love. He is awestruck and philosophical, seeing the pudenda as "the alpha and the omega". He kneels in worship, the kneeling being a necessary abasement before "a blessing come from heaven".

In the middle section, the singer is older and more jaundiced. He is "broken from bending", having "lived too long on my knees". His lover's nakedness is mere teasing now, and he turns in disgust from the fusion of love and hate that overwhelms him. (These two verses provide an excellent précis of most of the songs on his middle-period albums.)

In the final verses, Cohen has reconciled his earlier attitudes. He is wise enough to know that relationships can be problematic ("there's blood on every bracelet") and to see below surfaces ("don't forget there's still a woman / Beneath this resplendent chemise"). But he is not so wise that he forgets the 'cure' that carnal love offers, even if it is only effective "for something like a second".

ALWAYS

"Oh friends, don't matter if you're a man or a woman, if you're in love with somebody, these are the words that you gotta learn to say. Now listen carefully." Growling this introduction over background chatter, and fortified by a drink of his own invention known as Red Needle, Cohen launches into his version of Irving Berlin's classic number.

Cohen had known the song most of his life; it was a particular favourite of his mother's, and she would often sing it around the house. In the dance halls of his youth, it was the tune that signalled the moment to start dancing close as the evening came towards its end. He admired the song's structure and found the lyrics touching. Moreover, Cohen had some excellent musicians at hand who were up for a bit of fun; and fun is obviously what they had.

Whether Berlin would recognise his dainty little song is open to question. Set to a basic bar-band vamp, 'Always' was decorated, at various points, with a tasty blues guitar break, honky-tonk piano, and dance-band horns really giving it some welly. Cohen growls his way through an eight-minute version, hitting what is, along with the "babys" in 'Be For Real', surely his lowest recorded note along the way. He also adds (you can't keep a good poet down) a verse of his own, which exhibits in miniature the full range of his technique and style. "Not for just a second or a minute or an hour / Not for just a weekend and a shake-down in the shower / Not for just a summer and the winter going sour" is a long way from Berlin's delicate wordsmithery, and a fine and typical example of Cohen's.

TACOMA TRAILER

Never afraid to surprise us, Cohen ends the album with an instrumental track on which he does not himself perform. He originally wrote the music for a stage play and it is, in Devlin's words, "to all intents and purposes a right-handed piano solo over a low synth-strings accompaniment." It was "produced, programmed and performed" (as the credits put it) by Bill Ginn, with Steve Croes playing synclavier. It is a pleasant enough little number, almost a sorbet after the feast of the previous tracks, but no more nourishing than that.

TEN NEW SONGS

(First issued October 2001)

In 1999, having left the monastery at Mount Baldy where he had been living since 1994, Cohen began writing songs with Sharon Robinson, who had been a backing singer on his 1979 and 1980 tours and was a distinguished singer and songwriter in her own right. It was not their initial intention to make an album. "We just wanted to get together and write some songs" Cohen has said. In Robinson's words: "We just started working on things and it [the album] just happened".

Their working method was essentially that Cohen provided the lyrics, Robinson programmed a musical setting for them, and Cohen then recorded his vocals, though the process was more collaborative than that simple summary suggests. They worked, together or alone, in their home studios - credited on the album as Small Mercies Studio and Still Life Studios, though they were Robinson's garage and the study above Cohen's garage respectively. They considered replacing the electronic tracks with live musicians but, with the exception of Bob Metzger's guitar solo on 'In My Secret Life' and the strings on 'A Thousand Kisses Deep', they decided not to. Robinson reports that Cohen "liked the consistency of the record that we had and didn't want to spoil it".

That consistency is a notable feature of *Ten New Songs*, both in musical and thematic terms. It may lack the variation to be found in the body of Cohen's work taken as a whole, but no-one would criticise a painter because a painting did not include every colour on their palette. Neither Cohen nor Robinson were at the stage of their careers where they needed to use all their tricks at every appearance. *Ten New Songs* is a mature work by mature artists confident enough to do what was necessary to realise the songs and to avoid unnecessary embellishment.

IN MY SECRET LIFE

Cohen had begun work on this song as early as 1988, but the realised version sets the tone and style of the record that he and Robinson produced at turn of the millennium, with its slow and simple melody and its lyrical contrast between the internal and external worlds.

The "dealer" in the penultimate stanza is not, of course, a drug-culture reference. Rather he personifies those whose reported actions "make you want to cry"; in this context I am sure Cohen is thinking primarily of the businessman or politician. The final phrase - "it's crowded and cold / in my secret life" - is an intriguing observation by a poet who has inhabited and reported on both the social world and solitude.

A THOUSAND KISSES DEEP

A good example of the world-weariness and lyrical invention that permeate *Ten New Songs*, 'A Thousand Kisses Deep" is a musical and thematic companion-piece to 'Boogie Street' later on the album. "Invincible defeat" is a potent poetic paradox, and much of the song's imagery derives from the transgender sex bazaar that is Boogie Street by night.

'A Thousand Kisses Deep' is dedicated to Sandy Merriman (1945-1998), an American cancer-sufferer with whom Cohen had corresponded. He has said: "She was a woman in her middle fifties, and she committed suicide at a certain point. [She] indicated that my work kind of got her through the night. But, I guess it failed. I just wanted to keep her memory alive".

THAT DON'T MAKE IT JUNK

In the context of the album, 'That Don't Make It Junk" is a jaunty number, though it can hardly be described a upbeat. Cohen's penchant for paradox gets an airing in the phrase "I fought against the bottle / but I had to do it drunk". It is also a deft sketch of a persona Cohen has often adopted, the rebel against social (and indeed medical) convention.

An intriguing thought is that a key phrase of the chorus - "Took my diamond to the pawnshop / but that don't make it junk" - could be taken to refer to Cohen's abandonment of the "pure" literary life in favour of a career in popular music. While this change of direction is not a theme of the song, it certainly reflects Cohen's attitude to his career. Perhaps too there is an echo of the idea when he sings that he "closed the Book of Longing" (the title of a volume of poetry, prose and drawings that he subsequently published) in order to "do what I am told".

HERE IT IS

"Here is the love / that it's all built upon." Can there be a more eloquent description of a perennial Cohen theme, or indeed of his song-writing in general?

The song itself is a mature meditation on love ("that lists where it will") in the context of mortality and suffering, in a world of transience and sickness, with "your cross, your nails and your hill" (another and a good example of the use of religious imagery in a non-religious context), where death is "in the heart of your son" and "in your daughter's heart".

The structure of the song is an interesting reflection on the collaborative nature of the project that gave birth to the album. The song consists of four sets of two verses followed by a chorus. In each case, Sharon Robinson sings the first verse and she and Cohen duet on the second (and the chorus).

LOVE ITSELF

This is not a song that yields its meaning easily. The interaction between "the Nameless and the Name" and the recurrent motif of "the dust you seldom see" whose "flecks did float and dance" suggest this is no simple love song - indeed that its subject if not love, or at least not love in the carnal sense. It seems more likely that the song describes a spiritual journey. There is certainly a strong Buddhist flavour to the lyrics, and perhaps the denouement - when there is "nothing left between the Nameless and the Name" and "Love itself was gone" - represents the achieving of enlightenment.

The "LW" to whom the song is dedicated is the American writer Leon Wieseltier.

BY THE RIVERS DARK

This is a simple song with a complex subject, essentially the dualism of Cohen's relationship with the divine and the secular. "My lawless heart / and my wedding ring" eloquently express this dualism.

Babylon - a central image in the song - was a regional superpower in biblical times whose hostility to the Jews was most famously exhibited during the Babylonian Captivity, when the Jewish people where involuntarily transported and held there. . Babylon also features, in modern Rastafarian parlance, as a metaphor for the white-dominated and, in their view, morally bankrupt culture of the western world.

But although, in the song, Cohen lives "my life in Babylon", this does not condemn him to moral bankruptcy himself. "Though I take my song / from a withered limb / both song and tree / they sing for him." There are flowers in the desert.

ALEXANDRA LEAVING

'Alexandra Leaving' is a re-working of Constantine Cavafy's poem 'The God Abandons Antony'. Cavafy's poem is based on Plutarch's story that Mark Antony, besieged in Alexandria by Octavian, hears the sound of music passing through and out of the city and realises that it is the god Bacchus deserting him.

Cohen recasts the poem as a song about the end of a love affair. There are echoes of Cavafy's poem in the song - the leaving itself and a sense that the narrator lives a decadent life ("among the voices and the wine") that mirrors Mark Antony's sybaritic habits - but the theme of the song - stoicism in the face of love's disappointments - is Cohen's own. Indeed, it is a well-written late example of one of his regular themes.

YOU HAVE LOVED ENOUGH

On first hearing, 'You Have Loved Enough' seems a simple love song, with an elegant twist on Cohen's sense of victimhood - "it's love that seizes me". But we know enough of Cohen to doubt such apparent simplicity.

Given that Cohen spent several years living in Roshi's monastery in California immediately prior to writing *Ten New Songs*, one reading of the song is that it describes Cohen's spiritual journey as a full-time monk. The singer has "lost my job forever" and is "counted with the dead" - undoubtedly the contemporary view of the music business. He is given menial tasks by one who laughs at his ambition "to be your lover", who forbids delivery "when hatred with his package comes" , and who traffics in the verbal inversions common in Zen Buddhism - "I am not the one that loves / it's love that chooses me" and "you have loved enough / now let me be the Lover". (Note that it is "the" lover, not "your" lover, and that Cohen capitalises Lover in his printed lyrics - not conclusive evidence, but certainly suggesting that this is a spiritual not a carnal affair.)

But we know enough of Cohen to recognise his use of ambiguity and to avoid the temptation of a literal or a single interpretation.

BOOGIE STREET

The real 'Boogie Street' is Bugis Street in Singapore, by day a mainstream commercial and retail area but by night the centre of the transgender sex bazaar culture.

Cohen has described the metaphorical 'Boogie Street' as a "street of work and desire, the ordinary life and also the place we live in most of the time that is relieved by the embrace of your children, or the kiss of your beloved, or the peak experience in which you yourself are dissolved ... We all hope for those heavenly moments, which we get in those embraces and those sudden perceptions of beauty and sensations of pleasure, but we're immediately returned to Boogie Street".

Given the musical connotations of "boogie", perhaps one of Cohen's personal Boogie Streets Is his musical career (which has provided plenty of perceptions of beauty and sensations of pleasure), or more specifically life on tour, which has surely combined many professional days and louche nights over the years.

THE LAND OF PLENTY

With typical self-deprecation ("Don't have the courage to stand where I must stand / Don't really have the temperament to lend a helping hand"), Cohen offers an elegaic critique - more in sorrow than anger - of contemporary society, where there are "millions in the prison that wealth has set apart" and where "Christ has not risen from the caverns of the heart".

But 'The Land Of Plenty' is not a sociological analysis, but rather a prayer for the future - that the energy consumed by its lights may "shine on the truth some day".

DEAR HEATHER

(First issued October 2004)

Dear Heather, like *Ten New Songs*, was recorded in the Los Angeles home studios of Cohen and his long-time collaborator Sharon Robinson. Cohen's original intention was to call the album *Old Ideas*, but was persuaded that this might make potential customers think it was a compilation album and abandoned the idea.

The album lacks the unity of *Ten New Songs*. It includes some fully-realised songs, but others are more akin to sketches, and there are a number of songs written by others. It also gives prominence to other vocalists, notably Anjani Thomas (his current romantic partner), and features Cohen reciting as well as singing. Like all his recent albums, it was produced by Leanne Ungar, though Sharon Robinson, Anjani Thomas, Henry Lewy and Cohen himself also get production credits.

Given its patchwork nature, *Dear Heather* cannot be regarded as a significant Cohen album in the sense that it defines or develops a particular style or set of themes. It can perhaps best be regarded as offering a glimpse into the artist's sketchbook, showing, as it were, the draft outline rather than the completed oil painting. And as such it will be treasured by Cohen fans as an insight into his creative processes if not as a definitive masterpiece.

 GO NO MORE A-ROVING

The difference of approach from that of *Ten New Songs* is immediately signalled by the opening track, a setting of Lord Byron's poem sung by Cohen and Sharon Robinson over simple musical backing featuring the tenor sax of Bob Sheppard.

The song is dedicated to Irving Layton, an old (and older) friend and fellow poet from the Montreal literary scene of his youth who was seriously ill with Alzheimers Disease at the time of recording.

 BECAUSE OF

'Because Of' is an intriguing song. It is apparently simply, three verses sung twice by Cohen (the first time more recitation than singing and the second with significantly different phrasing) with the final verse repeated by Anjani Thomas (with some backing assistance from Cohen). It appears a somewhat boastful song, hymning his success with women - surely an attitude more suited to an adolescent than to one "in my old age".

But it is clearly not sexual conquest of which he is boasting. And there is an interesting poetic contrast between the women becoming "naked in their different ways" and their covering Cohen up "like a baby that is shivering". There is clearly more to the song than first appears, though it is nonetheless a slight piece compared to his more fully realised songs.

THE LETTERS

Co-written by Sharon Robinson, 'The Letters' is similar in style and tone to the songs they wrote together for *Ten New Songs*. Robinson also sings on the song, which is marked by a stylistic trick that Cohen uses several times on the album - repeating the lyrics in full a second time.

The division of vocal duties between Cohen and Robinson suggests an intriguing interpretation of the lyrics. When she sings the verse beginning "Your story was so long, the plot was so intense" are we to infer that "she" is the recipient of the letters, responding to the "writer" than Cohen voices? If so, then the years it took "to cross the lines of self-defence" refers to Cohen, not his correspondent, and any criticism is directed at himself, not at her.

UNDERTOW

Over a smoky sax backing, Anjani Thomas sings the lyric. It gives a different nuance to the words when they are sung by a woman ("with a child in my arms and a chill in my soul") than when sung by a man, though the song as a whole is not gender-specific. Cohen repeats the lyric, though he whispers rather than sings it, at the end.

MORNING GLORY

Cohen recites rather than sings the main lyrics, overdubbing himself to give a curiously dislocated, atmospheric feel to the piece. The final words ("Oh the morning glory") are sung by Anjani Thomas.

'Morning Glory' is closer in approach to the poetry readings backed by jazz musicians that Cohen took part in during his Montreal youth than to the songs of his "main career" as a singer-songwriter, though the style is some way distant from that of the 50's jazz & poetry world. The poem may be a slight piece, but it lends itself well to the treatment it is given and one can understand why Cohen chose to work on it and include it in the miscellany that is *Dear Heather*.

ON THAT DAY

'On That Day', by contrast, is a "proper" song, co-written by Anjani Thomas (who also plays piano on the recorded version). Unusually in Cohen's oeuvre, it is directly concerned with a recent political event, the attack on New York by airborne terrorists on 11 September 2001.

The final stanza asks "did you go crazy or did you report" and it is interesting that the sleeve notes include an extract from *The American Heritage Dictionary* defining "report" as "*v., -intr.,* 3. To present oneself: report for duty", an unusual example of Cohen eschewing ambiguity.

VILLANELLE FOR OUR TIME

As a poet, Cohen is not noted for his use of strict poetic structures, so it is something of a departure for him to perform an example of one of the most intricate poetic forms, albeit one written by Frank Scott.

The performance begins as a simple recitation, with a musical backing entering during the third verse. Cohen repeats verses two, four and six, with Anjani Thomas singing behind his recitation, then twice repeats verse two and the final line, before concluding with verses five and six. (So even when performing an example of one of the most intricate verse forms, Cohen is no slave to convention!)

'Villanelle For Our Time' was recorded in May 1999, shortly after Cohen left the Mount Baldy monastery.

THERE FOR YOU

Co-written by Sharon Robinson, this was their third collaboration on *Dear Heather*. Again, it would not have sounded out of place on *Ten New Songs*.

If addressed to an individual woman, this song would simply be flattering or romantic. Given what we know about the complexities of Cohen's work and the richness of his love-life, it is surely a better reading to see it as addressed to womankind in general, or to the abstract Love, whose servant Cohen has ever been.

 ### DEAR HEATHER

The title track is the shortest lyric in Cohen's songbook, sketching its subject with all the deftness of a Zen painter's single stroke.

Over plinky-plonky la-la's, decorated by Sarah Kramer's trumpet-playing, Cohen recites the lyric over and over, in a strange jerky style, on many occasions spelling out the letters of a word rather than saying it. The effect is bizarre but mesmerising, more the product of a laboratory than a library, and a tribute to Cohen's willingness to experiment even (or especially) so late in his career.

 ### NIGHTINGALE

By contrast a conventional song, co-written by Anjani Thomas, 'Nightingale' is a beautiful lament for to a departed singer. It was dedicated to Carl Anderson, the singer and actor, who had recently died.

Played jauntily, belying but not undermining the elegaic nature of the lyrics, the song has a lovely melody and some of Cohen's finest and most compassionate words. Although clearly tied to a specific loss, it is not anchored to a single story, and stands as a lament for loss in general, allowing the listener to apply it to their own circumstances and doing what poetry does at its best - making an individual experience general.

 ### TO A TEACHER

Another elegy, but in a very different style. 'To A Teacher' is dedicated to Abraham Moses Klein, a Canadian writer best known as a poet and cited by Cohen as an early influence. Klein was a significant figure on the Montreal literary scene from the Thirties onwards, and an important member of the Montreal Jewish community. After 1956, he gave up writing and became a recluse, the "silence" referred to in the song's opening words.

The words were originally published in *The Spice-Box of Earth*. This was the first time for many years that Cohen had recycled one of his earlier poems into a song, though he had often done so at the start of his career.

 ### THE FAITH

'The Faith' was a new song written to the tune of 'Un Canadien Errant', which Cohen had covered on *Recent Songs*. Indeed, the basic track was an out-take from the *Recent Songs* sessions, with Raffi Hakopian on violin, John Bilezikijan on oud, Bill Ginn on piano, Roscoe Beck on bass, Paul Ostermayer on flute, Mitch Watkins on guitar and Garth Hudson on accordion. For this reason, Henry Lewy, the producer of *Recent Songs* earned a co-production credit for *Dear Heather*, despite the fact that he was long retired and in poor health.

 ### TENNESSEE WALTZ

The original song was written in 1947 by Redd Stewart and Pee Wee King, and was a favourite in both the country and popular music genres. Cohen added a third verse when he performed the song on 9 July 1985 at the Montreux Jazz Festival. The version on *Dear Heather* is a digitally cleaned up radio recording of the performance.

OLD IDEAS

(First issued 2012)

This time, Cohen was not dissuaded from using the title *Old Ideas* and his twelfth studio album, released in January 2012 to critical acclaim and commercial success, was so called.

The album is notable for the wide range of collaborators with whom Cohen worked, including some long-standing artistic partners like Sharon Robinson and Anjani Thomas, and others, like Patrick Leonard, who were "new friends". Of course, collaborative working was not a new departure but something Cohen had been doing for years, but it is an intriguing denouement for someone who started his musical journey as that archetypal lone wolf, the singer-songwriter.

Old Ideas is a more substantial album than its predecessor *Dear Heather* and, perhaps inevitably given the number of different collaborators he worked with, more stylistically varied than *Ten New Songs*. In many ways, it encapsulates much of Cohen's more recent studio work – it includes songs that can hold their own in the canon of his work and would not have sounded out of place on his 2008-10 World Tour, and others that are slighter and more sketch-like.

It is too early, at the time of writing, to offer a final judgement on the album's place in the pantheon of Cohen's work. My instinct is that few people will come to see it as Cohen's greatest album but that for most it will be one of the albums to be considered when making that choice.

GOING HOME

The album opens with the first of four collaborations with Patrick Leonard, who "wrote, produced, arranged, engineered, programmed and performed the music" with assistance from Dana Glover who arranged and sang "the women's parts".

Over a slow and pretty melody, Cohen growls – it can hardly be said he sings – lyrics that are both startling and puzzling. The start is provided by Cohen's self-description as "a lazy bastard living in a suit"; the puzzle is to determine who the singer's character is. The main narrator appears not to be Cohen himself – he "wants to speak with Leonard" and has told him what to complete and to repeat. But the singer of the chorus uses the first person – "my sorrow", "my burden", "the costume that I wore" – in a context that suggests these are Cohen's own words. So who is the other voice?

An intriguing possibility is that it is Cohen's long-time spiritual guide Roshi – certainly the turn of phrase echoes his style, and the sentiments have the spikiness appropriate to a Buddhist abbot. Or perhaps it would be more reasonable to say it is Cohen's own expression of his teacher's instructions, making the song the expression of an internal dialogue (much as 'Famous Blue Raincoat' was many years earlier). The debate is between his work – "he wants to write a love song... a manual for living with defeat" (incidentally as good a critical summary of his oeuvre as one could find) – and his spiritual path – shedding his burden of sorrow and "going home to where it's better than before".

AMEN

This collaboration with Sharon Robinson is a classic example of "a love song… a manual for living with defeat" – "tell me again when I'm clean and I'm sober / tell me again when I've seen through the horror" sees Cohen back on some very familiar territory. Indeed, with its rich language and varied musicality, it is easy to imagine the song being performed on the World Tour.

Cohen also revives one of his old linguistic tricks – the use of religious vocabulary in a secular context. Here we have angels "panting and scratching the door to come in" and "the filth of the butcher [being] washed in the blood of the lamb" as well, of course, as the song's very title. But it is a love song or, more accurately, a plea for love – "tell me again / tell me over and over / tell me that you want me".

 ### SHOW ME THE PLACE

'Show Me The Place' is the second collaboration with Patrick Leonard. This time, Cohen's old cohort Jennifer Warnes provides the "women's parts", and there is a lovely violin passage played by Bela Santelli.

So what is the place that Cohen asks to be shown? Given his history of writing about a man's love for a woman, we might guess that he is talking (and in this case with something of a masochistic bent) about "women's parts" - the place "where the Word became a man" and "where the suffering began". But Cohen has not often written about the mechanics of sex and has not noticeably mined a gynaecological vein in his other work. So we might rather suspect he is talking about a more metaphorical place – a stance, a position or a relationship. It might even refer to a spiritual destination, the term "slave" echoing his spiritual master.

Not for the first time, Cohen the poet is using ambiguity. Not for the first time, he is using it with some success.

 ### DARKNESS

Cohen recorded 'Darkness' with the band (identified here as the United Heart Touring Band) that accompanied him to such great effect on his World Tour. Indeed the song was performed during the latter stages of that tour. A blues-based song (including such an old blues motif as the repeated opening line), it is the nearest he is likely to get to a stomping rocker.

'Darkness' is a bleak song, echoing the attitude of much of The Future. Indeed, if he had then "seen the future, brother, it is murder", now that future seems to have arrived – "the present's not that pleasant … I got no taste for anything at all". And there is an oblique reference to his much publicised money troubles – "I thought the past would last me / but the darkness got that too".

So does the song belie Cohen's statements that, as he has got older, his life-long depression has lifted? Maybe. But maybe we would be wise to distinguish the character who sings from the real man. After all, the singer claims: "I don't smoke no cigarette / I don't drink no alcohol / I ain't had much loving yet". Aside from being less grammatically elegant than Cohen usually is, these statements do not fit the known facts of his life. So we may conclude that 'Darkness' is a song, not an autobiography.

ANYHOW

If with 'Darkness' we are in a concert hall, with 'Anyhow' we are in a lounge bar. Patrick Leonard's decorative piano so conjures up such an environment that one can almost hear the tired clink of glasses as the weary evening draws to an unhappy close. This is no raucous 'Closing Time' but a downbeat "end of the affair". Cohen growls his plea to his erstwhile lover. We know of course (he has told us so himself) that "a man never got a woman back... by begging on his knees" – but Cohen is not begging her to return. Rather, he wants her "mercy", wants her to moderate the violence of her negative emotions – "I know you have to hate me / but could you hate me less?" I think most of his fans would hope that she can.

CRAZY TO LOVE YOU

'Crazy To Love You' was co-written with Anjani Thomas, his sometime romantic partner, though it is unclear whether or not the affair the song delineates is theirs.

It is a curious song, not least linguistically. The singer "had to go crazy to love you" (not, note, the caustically unromantic "had to be crazy") and the tenor of the song suggests that this was an act of volition rather than an involuntary succumbing to mental illness. Later, "crazy" is used as a noun - "begging my crazy to quit" and "crazy has places to hide in". It is certainly a neologistic usage, without any lexicographical sanction, but if taken as a synonym for "madness" makes sense.

What makes less sense is the scenario the song describes. Why did the singer have to beg his crazy to quit? When he chases his lover ("you") "through the souvenir heartaches / her braids and her blouse all undone", who is the third person in such a state of dishabille? And why, if "you... were never the one", did the singer need to go to such lengths to love her? We have often praised Cohen's use of ambiguity, but perhaps this song is simply unclear and imperfectly realised.

COME HEALING

The album's fourth and final collaboration with Patrick Leonard, 'Come Healing' is indeed, as it describes itself, a "penitential hymn". As on 'Going Home' and 'Anyhow', the female voices are arranged and sung by Dana Glover. Here, she sings the first verse solo and, after a solo stanza from Cohen, duets with him for the rest of the song.

This is another of Cohen's songs of compassion in a world of "brokenness" and "troubled dust" where "none of us [deserve] the cruelty or the grace", but wherein "the branches [long] to lift the little bud" and "the arteries to purify the blood". And it is a unifying healing he seeks – of body and mind, of spirit and limb, of reason and heart. 'Come Healing' is the shortest song on the album but, though small, is perfectly formed.

BANJO

Collaborating again with Sharon Robinson and set to a lilting country melody, 'Banjo' is nevertheless quite unlike any of Cohen's other songs. He has written songs that are ambiguous or difficult to interpret, but never one with such an hallucinatory feel – not a drug-induced hallucination but the weird logic of dreams.

Are we really to believe that the "broken banjo bobbing" (wonderful alliteration with a distinct out-of-this-world flavour) is an object of great significance to Cohen? How precisely might a wave wash a banjo "out of someone's grave", and what was banjo doing there in the first place? Why is it duty-bound to harm him? Who has imposed such a duty on an inanimate piece of flotsam? How might it discharge this duty?

I doubt there are rational answers to these questions. But in a dream, the statements would make perfect sense. I think we are dealing with, so to speak, a piece of abstract rather than representational art – not with a literal or metaphorical exposition of beliefs or philosophy but rather with the creation of a mood. And very well evoked it is too.

LULLABY

After the somewhat nightmarish visions of 'Banjo', Cohen soothes us with 'Lullaby', a song that does exactly what it says on the tin. Here is no philosophical disquisition, no anatomisation of the relationships between men and women, no searing indictment of the world and its horrors, simply a tender song in simple language beautifully realised.

Sharon Robinson sings the female vocals (solo for the first line of the chorus) and plays synth bass. Ed Sanders branches out from his producer role to play some guitar and to arrange and sing the men's choral parts.

DIFFERENT SIDES

To close the album, Cohen returns to one of his perennial themes, what he had years earlier referred to as the "war between the man and the woman". It may not be a war that either party wants to prosecute, and it may not be important in the scheme of things, but in the mundane, quotidian world we actually inhabit, it is real: "We find ourselves on different sides / of a line that nobody drew / though it all may be one in the higher eye / down here where we live it is two".

The song includes a marvellously witty summation of many an argument: "I say that you shouldn't you couldn't you can't / you say that you must and you will". But if Cohen is casting himself as a war reporter, it is his lover who is the keener journalist – she wants to "live where the suffering is" and clearly irks him by "writing everything down". Cohen would rather "get out of town".

But Cohen wouldn't be Cohen if he didn't "live where the suffering is" and he is not above a little knowing self-caricature. "By virtue of suffering I claim to have won" could be the motto of his entire career.

PART II
LIVE ALBUMS

LEONARD COHEN : LIVE SONGS

LIVE SONGS

(First issued April 1973)

Cohen's first live album was compiled and released in the interval between *Songs Of Love And Hate* and *New Skin For The Old Ceremony*. Produced, like his two previous studio albums, by Bob Johnston, *Live Songs* was mixed from recordings made during Cohen's two previous tours, two songs being taken from the 1970 tour and eight from the tour of 1972.

Although the album offers a pretty representative sampling of his live show at the time (Cohen has stated that "it documents this phase [of my career] very clearly"), it was poorly received and was not a commercial success. Part of the reason may lie in Cohen's state of mind in the early Seventies, as evidenced by his later comment that the album "represented a very confused and directionless time" in his life. Another reason, perhaps not unconnected to the first, was the unhelpful publicity arising from an interview Cohen gave to *Melody Maker* reporter Roy Hollingworth, in which he expressed his disillusionment with the music business.

Hollingworth quoted Cohen as saying that "I just cannot stand to remain part of the business" and expressing a wish "no longer... to be tangled up in the mechanisms" of the industry. These statements were interpreted as a decision to retire. Although Cohen denied this, claiming he had explicitly told Hollingworth "I don't want to see a headline:

Leonard Cohen quits music business and goes into monastery", the damage had been done, not least to his reputation within the industry. In Hollingworth's defence, it is clear that he correctly reflected Cohen's general sentiments. It was also a little naïve of Cohen to expect a working journalist to ignore such a meaty story laid on his plate during a professional encounter.

The unhappy emotions swirling round the release of *Live Songs* were exacerbated by the inclusion of sleevenotes written by the little-known (and mentally unstable) artist and poet Daphne Richardson. Her quoted statement that a "mad mystic hammering of your body upon my body" amounted to a "union... that almost killed me with its INTENSITY" was rendered tragically poignant by her suicide three days before Cohen was to offer her a contract to illustrate his latest volume of poetry.

 MINUTE PROLOGUE
Recorded at the Royal Albert Hall in London on 23 March 1972, the only known occasion when Cohen has performed it, 'Minute Prologue' (as in "sixty seconds" rather than "very small", though the ambiguity serves its poetic purpose) is a bleak and sombre song. "I've been listening to all the dissension, I've been listening to all the pain", he sings. But Cohen's apparently hopeful conclusion that "I think I can heal it with this song" – on first hearing, a tribute to the redemptive power of music – is undermined by his assertion, inserted into the final repetition of the line, that he is a fool to think so. In opening the album thus, Cohen does seem to be embracing his miserabilism.

PASSING THROUGH

Recorded during the same concert as 'Minute Prologue', 'Passing Through' was written by Richard Blakeslee, although Cohen claims an arranger's credit for this version. A song that might have been included in *The People's Songbook* that Cohen had sung from in his teens, 'Passing Through' situates Cohen in the folksinging mainstream, perhaps past its peak by 1972 but still a recognisable and popular genre. The song namechecks Jesus Christ, Adam (of Garden of Eden fame), George Washington and Franklin Roosevelt, and exhibits all the vaguely left-wing sentiments of the so-called protest movement exemplified musically by Peter, Paul & Mary, Joan Baez and, in his earliest incarnation, Bob Dylan. "Yankee, Russian, white or tan / A man is just a man", a statement the song attributes to President Roosevelt, is a typical (and admirable) indication of where the song's heart lies.

Although this version is the only one Cohen has released, the song has made occasional appearances on his tours up to and including 1993.

YOU KNOW WHO I AM

This version was recorded at the Ancienne Belgique concert hall in Brussels on 16 April 1972. It follows substantially the original arrangement used on *Song From A Room*, although the Jew's harp of the studio version has been replaced by some ethereal keyboard work from Bob Johnston and some descant harmonies from backing singers Jennifer Warnes and Donna Washburn. The tempo seems slower than that of the original, though this may be an illusion created by its greater length (at 5:22 it is almost two minutes longer), since the original itself was taken at no great pace.

BIRD ON THE WIRE

Performing in Paris at the Salle Pleyel on 18 April 1972 gave Cohen a chance to demonstrate the bilingualism he had learnt in his native Montreal by introducing in French this version of one of his most famous songs. Again, the arrangement is largely faithful to the original studio version, albeit with a slightly richer guitar melody.

Oddly, given the song's prominence in Cohen's catalogue, the lyrics were not honoured with the same fidelity. The linguistically awkward and somewhat twee claim that the singer has "saved all my ribbons for thee" is replaced by the darker observation that "it was the shape of our love [that] twisted me". A similarly bleak, though perhaps more honest, emendation follows the phrase "if I have been untrue". No longer does Cohen "hope you know it was never to you", a hope that events had surely rendered unrealistic. Instead, his excuse is now that "I thought a lover had to be some kind of liar too", though this elevation of practice into theory does strike a rather self-justificatory note.

One must respect a poet's right to edit their work, however well known the original may be. On the other hand, one is entitled to conclude that the changes made in this case do alter the tone of the song. It is now more cynical and more bitter, than the lyrical, perhaps even naïve, earlier version. One can see this even where Cohen has not altered the original words. For instance, in the "beggar/pretty woman" quatrain, although the basic words remain unchanged, they are delivered in a more improvised style – repeating phrases and inserting "come-on-nows" – that dilutes the original poetic precision to no great purpose.

That Cohen himself did not think the new version of the song was entirely successful may perhaps be deduced from the further changes that, as we shall see, he was to make some years later.

NANCY

This version of 'Seems So Long Ago, Nancy' from *Songs From A Room* was recorded at the same Royal Albert Hall gig as 'Minute Prologue' and 'Passing Through'. The shortened title reflects a change to the song's opening words. On the album, it began "It seems so long ago". Here, the opening line is "The morning had not come". This relatively minor change, which does not alter the song's essential story line, does bring about a shift in its focus. As well as adding descriptive colour to the portrayal of Nancy's loneliness, the change also removes the singer from the action. It is no longer a reminiscence. The audience can therefore concentrate on the portrait of dysfunctional misery the song presents. When, at its conclusion, Cohen brings the audience into the song ("Why don't you look around you" and "Many of you used her body"), the shock of the challenge is all the greater. One cannot but admire the poetic economy with which Cohen has achieved this change of emphasis in what is otherwise a virtually unchanged song.

IMPROVISATION

'Improvisation' is in fact the instrumental backing for the song 'You Know Who I Am', recorded at the same Salle Pleyel concert as the version of 'Bird On The Wire' two tracks previously (and two days after the full version of 'You Know Who I Am' included as track three). It is a pleasant enough interlude, though somewhat lacking in substance. The melody meanders along amiably, but there is no significant development of the theme; the track is an instrumental workout rather than a piece in its own right.

'Improvisation' is of greatest interest when compared with the piece from which it is taken, 'You Know Who I Am'. On its own, the music is pretty and melodic, if not especially inspiring. It is not obvious that this is a Leonard Cohen number. When combined with the lyrics, however, the music recedes into the background, its prettiness counterpointing the more astringent vocal melody to produce a song that is recognisably Cohen's.

STORY OF ISAAC

Recorded on 8 April 1972 at the Sportpalast in Berlin, the live version of 'Story of Isaac' differs little from the studio one included on *Songs From A Room*. Cohen introduces the song as being "about those who would sacrifice one generation on behalf of another", an earlier version of his comments quoted above when discussing the studio version.

PLEASE DON'T PASS ME BY (A DISGRACE)

'Please Don't Pass Me By' is an extremely unusual Cohen song. In the context of *Live Songs*, it stands out for its length – 13 minutes, more than twice the length of any other, and three times longer than most. As a song, it is unusual in its structure, consisting of a simple repeated chorus interspersed with ad-libbed spoken sections. The chorus itself is a 'found poem', the key lines ("Please don't pass me by / For I am blind and you can see / I've been blinded totally") being taken straight from a New York City beggar's cardboard placard. Moreover, unlike most Cohen songs, where the literary and musical elements stand up on their own, this song is essentially a performance piece; naked on the cold page it is nothing.

This version was recorded at London's Royal Albert Hall on 10 May 1970. It closed the show, thus allowing Cohen to improvise several repetitions of the basic chorus, each cranking his – and the audience's – emotions another notch up the scale. It is known that he was later embarrassed by the intensity of his performance. Late in the song, he shouts that "I can't stand myself" and confesses to being both a tyrant and a slave (a typically Cohenesque conjunction). It is said that he was later ashamed of letting himself go under the withering gaze of Prince Albert's statue. Interestingly but perhaps not surprisingly, this was the last occasion on which he performed this song.

TONIGHT WILL BE FINE

This is the second song that Cohen committed to disc from his set at the 1970 Isle of Wight Festival, following 'Sing Another Song, Boys' which had been included on *Songs Of Love And Hate*. The original version of this song had appeared on *Songs From A Room*, but here a different arrangement is used. It has, thanks in the main to Bubba Fowler's banjo, a much more countrified, hoe-down feel.

This gives a very different feeling to the live version. Gone is the tuneful seductiveness of the original, setting up by its sweetness the "for a while" sting in the song's tail. Now the whole song seems infused by a bitter sarcasm, which draws rather than sharpens its sting. The two additional verses increase this feeling, describing as they do Cohen's own state of mind and making no reference to the woman addressed in the original version. Cohen is down on his luck and not afraid to share his self-pity with us. "The cards that they dealt me, there weren't any aces / And the horses never listen to me at the races" may not be the most elegant lines he has ever penned, but we may certainly concur with Dorman and Rawlins that they "develop the mood of abandonment and all-round dejection".

 ### QUEEN VICTORIA

This is a 'live song' only in the most elastic sense of the term. The song is essentially a setting to music of the poem 'Queen Victoria And Me' from *Flowers For Hitler*, and was recorded in a cabin in Tennessee on a tape recorder lent to the singer by Bob Johnston. Cohen has never even performed the song in public. Its only claim to being 'live' is that the singer sang it at the moment of recording!

We have seen before that Cohen is no very exact historian, and his characterisation of the young Queen Victoria as a "slim unlovely virgin floating among German beer" would have startled contemporaries of this highly-sexed daughter of the notoriously lecherous House of Hanover. Indeed, it was the very carnal enjoyment she derived from her marriage to Prince Albert that sharpened her widow's mourning.

But historical accuracy is not Cohen's purpose. Rather, it is the "solitary mourner of a prince" with her "incomparable sense of loss" with whom he identifies. Cohen's Victoria is his alter ego, mirroring and sharing his own solitary sadness, not the portrait of a nineteenth-century monarch. As a song, however, the piece does not really work. The tune is mournful and barely melodic, and the lyrics seem mannered and over-literary compared to most of Cohen's songs.

LIVE IN CONCERT

(First issued July 1994)

Cohen's second live album (sometimes known by the short title *Cohen Live* and occasionally, where the context demands, as *Leonard Cohen Live In Concert*) offers thirteen songs taken from his 1988 and 1993 tours. It was mixed and mastered in Los Angeles, and co-produced by Leanne Ungar (who had co-produced his previous studio album, *The Future*) and Bob Metzger (guitarist on both the tours).

Both in style and content, *Live In Concert* gives a fair reflection of Cohen's contemporary touring act. He himself has said that it "represents the final pages of a chapter [that] began with *Various Positions* and *I'm Your Man* and *The Future*; these are old songs re-fashioned". Seven of the songs do indeed come from his first four albums, the remaining six being of more recent vintage. We can assume that Cohen felt that songs from *The Future*, issued the previous year, were too recent to include. The set is thus drawn in almost equal measure from his early and late periods. The 'missing' albums are *Death Of A Ladies' Man* (unsurprisingly, given the traumas of its creation) and *Recent Songs* (more surprisingly, though stylistically it is neither 'ancient' nor 'modern').

The release of *Live In Concert* met with a mixed critical reception, though it is fair to say that by this stage in Cohen's career, reactions tended to follow pre-determined lines. (The *Time* critic who wrote that the album "should be dispensed only with large doses of Prozac" must, however, have been of an unusually nervous disposition.) It is a reasonable conclusion that *Live In Concert* has neither gained nor lost Cohen any fans.

DANCE ME TO THE END OF LOVE

This version is one of five songs on the album taken from Cohen's concert at the O'Keefe Centre in Toronto on 17 June 1993. (Another comes from the following night at the same venue.) 'Dance Me To The End Of Love' was Cohen's normal concert opener in both 1988 and 1993, displacing 'Bird On The Wire' which had formerly held that honour.

It is also the first of four songs from *Various Positions*. The arrangement is substantially the same as on that album, though taken slightly more *con brio* and decorated with some soaring violin work from Bob Furgo.

BIRD ON THE WIRE

A second number from the same concert as 'Dance Me To The End Of Love', this version of one of Cohen's most famous songs is given the full band treatment. Cohen is in growlier voice than ever and, after the first two verses (which follow the 1973 text used on *Live Songs*), we are treated to breaks by Bob Metzger on guitar and then Paul Ostermayer on sax.

At this point – some four minutes in – the song pauses, restarting at a slower tempo. The usual third verse follows; then, instead of the "beggar/pretty woman" quatrain, Cohen gives us a new verse before finishing with the standard ending, a repetition of the first three lines. The new verse ("don't cry... it's over, it's finished, it's completed, it's been paid for") is certainly in line with the style and sentiments of Cohen's songs of the Nineties. However, it is hard to see how it improves on the original, and harder still to see how it fits with the rest of the song. From an artistic perspective, the new verse seems to me an emendation too far.

EVERYBODY KNOWS

This version was recorded later on the North American segment of the 1993 tour, at Vancouver's Orpheum Theatre on 29 July. The treatment is in general very similar to that on *I'm Your Man*, though Cohen offers some minor variations to the main vocal line and, on stage, the band seems to play more heavily and to swing less fluently than it did in the studio. The studio version remains a more definitive reading of the song.

 JOAN OF ARC

The third song recorded at the O'Keefe Centre on 17 June 1993, this version of 'Joan Of Arc' is sung as a duet with Julie Christensen. By comparing this version with the one on Jennifer Warnes' album *Famous Blue Raincoat*, where she and Cohen alternate the different parts, one can see much more clearly than when Cohen sings it alone that the song has four characters.

In the first verse, Cohen begins as the Narrator (a part Warnes sang on her own album); Christensen then comes in as Joan (as Warnes did). In the second verse, Cohen continues as the Narrator (he had sung this segment on Warnes' album), before Christensen enters as Joan, handing back to Cohen in the role of Fire. The third verse starts with Christensen as Joan, ending with Cohen as the Narrator (the same pattern as on *Famous Blue Raincoat*). Cohen sings all of the final verse. However, noting that the final lines are italicised in the sleevenotes, one becomes aware that these lines are sung by a fourth character. The Bystander ends the song by enunciating the tragic dilemma which he faces: "myself, I long for love and light / But must it come so cruel, must it be so bright?"

Allied to the poignantly lyrical and romantic backing (Bob Furgo's violin must be mentioned in dispatches here), this double-handed treatment of the song draws out its full complexity and makes this the definitive version of the song Cohen has produced.

 THERE IS A WAR

Yet another song from the 17 June gig in Toronto, 'There Is A War' is given a much rockier, almost danceable, backing than the original. But it was not a very good song when it first appeared, and has improved little with age and repackaging.

 SISTERS OF MERCY

Also recorded at Toronto's O'Keefe Centre, though this time on 18 July, this live version shows just what Cohen and his Nineties band can do with a classic song. The basic arrangement is little changed from the famous original, though it is here scored for a full band. Nonetheless, the mood of the original – tender, wistful and romantic – is faithfully re-created. The additions of instrumental breaks from Paul Ostermayer (on sax) and Bob Furgo (on violin) enhance this mood with exquisite lyricism. Cohen's voice is, of course, now several notches lower than it was in the Sixties, but it works with this material just as well as his old one did. Contrasting the two versions of this song shows both how far he has travelled in the meantime, not least musically, and yet how much he is still recognisably the same artist he always was. The treatment of this song offered here is a timely reminder that in the sphere of songwriting, as in many others, class will out.

 HALLELUJAH

Although this version was recorded (on 31 October 1988 at the *Austin City Limits* TV Studio in Austin, Texas) only four years after the original appeared on *Various Positions*, the lyrics are almost entirely different. The fourth and final verse remains unchanged, but the first three are completely new. Gone is the "baffled king" David, and with him most of the religious elements of the song. Its psalm-like mood remains, but it is now applied to a purely secular purpose.

In this incarnation, the song deals with a perennial Cohen theme – the loneliness of love's failure. To this he adds a stoical and philosophical acceptance to draw the poison of his despair: "and even though it all went wrong / I'll stand before the Lord of Song / With nothing on my lips but Hallelujah!" Poetically, the new verses meet Cohen's highest standards. "I used to live alone before I knew you", a simple phrase unburdened with elaborate poeticism, not only deftly implies the weight of hope that new love bears but also (mere technical requirements but important to a poet nonetheless) both scans and hits a difficult rhyme. The line "but all I ever learned from love / Was how to shoot at someone who outdrew you" elicits, not for the first time in Cohen's work, the shiver of authentic poetry.

That the song is beautifully sung and accompanied seems almost a bonus.

 ### I'M YOUR MAN
The album's final cut from the Toronto concert on 17 June 1993, this version of 'I'm Your Man' follows closely the one on the eponymous album released five years earlier, though obviously it has been orchestrated for the tour band. The original lyrics are substantially adhered to, but Cohen is clearly playing to the crowd. To cheers from the audience, he inserts some additional adjectives – "if you want another kind of love / I'll wear my *leather* mask for you" and "if you want a *Jewish* doctor / I'll examine every inch of you". For all his seriousness of artistic purpose, Cohen is, after all, up on stage to entertain us.

 ### WHO BY FIRE
Recorded, like 'Hallelujah', for a TV show in Austin, Texas, Cohen faithfully reproduces the lyrics and melody line of the original version on *New Skin For The Old Ceremony*. The band, however, departs somewhat from that version, opening with a middle-eastern-sounding intro, backing Cohen's singing in similar fashion, before closing out the song with two more minutes in the same vein.

 ### ONE OF US CANNOT BE WRONG
This version was recorded during a televised show at the Velódromo De Anoeta in San Sebastian on 20 May 1988. One of the oldest songs in his set list, 'One Of Us Cannot Be Wrong' has been "re-fashioned" for modern concert performance, but it is still recognisably the same song. Cohen takes, as he is entitled to, some liberties with the phrasing of the vocals but, because he is obviously so familiar with the song, they enhance rather than detract from the performance. The lyrics printed in the sleevenotes are unchanged, but on stage Cohen adds a telling adjective when singing of "the details of our shabby honeymoon". All in all, the song holds up well to its more contemporary treatment.

 ### IF IT BE YOUR WILL
The third selection from the *Austin City Limits* TV show recorded on 31 October 1988, Cohen sings 'If It Be Your Will', if not exactly solo, then at least without the full band behind him. Apart from a murmur of keyboards later in the song and the accompaniment of his regular backing singers, Perla Batalla and Julie Christensen, Cohen reverts to his "singer with guitar" stance of former years. This suits the reverential, hymn-like qualities of the song and he gives a fine performance, though one that is necessarily similar to the original version on *Various Positions*.

HEART WITH NO COMPANION

By contrast, 'Heart With No Companion' from the same album is given a much jollier treatment than its original. Bob Furgo's violin sets up a country rhythm that drives the whole band along. If this is slightly at odds with the tenor of the song's lyrics, with their compassionate depiction of various states of loss (the shipless captain, the childless mother, etc.), it suitably defines a mood "on the other side of sorrow and despair".

This is the earliest of the recordings included on the album, having been performed on 19 April 1988 at the Muziek Theatre in Amsterdam.

SUZANNE

This version of the first song on Cohen's first album was recorded (like 'Everybody Knows') at the Orpheum Theatre in Vancouver on 29 July 1993, the penultimate night of his last tour. Though, as in the original, the backing is dominated by the song's famous guitar riff, it is played deeper and sounds more fragile, as does Cohen's voice. This is a darker, sadder reading of the song than he had offered previously. Indeed, he had not at first wanted to include it on the album. "When it came to 'Suzanne', I didn't want to put it on there because there's so much invested in the whole thing. But they said 'It's where you are, Leonard. It's broken, it's true, it's deconstructed, it's... you.' " And if one must not read a complete biography into a single performance of a single song, it is undoubtedly true that only one man could have written this song, or given this performance of it.

FIELD COMMANDER COHEN: TOUR OF 1979

(First issued February 2001)

Recorded at the Hammersmith Odeon, London on 4, 5 and 6 December and at the Dome Theatre on 15 December 1979, *Field Commander Cohen* documents the tour Cohen undertook shortly after the release of *Recent Songs*, from which four songs are included on the live album.

Cohen was accompanied on tour by the band Passenger, the violinist Raffi Hakopian and the oudist John Bilezikjian, who had all played on the *Recent Songs* sessions, with backing vocals by Jennifer Warnes and a young Sharon Robinson. Cohen is reported to have regarded the tour as his best to date, and it certainly reflects a period when he was starting to regain his creative credibility, though his commercial recovery would take somewhat longer.

The album is dedicated to the memory of John Wood (1950-1983), who is described in the sleeve notes as "the technical member of Passenger" and (in a quote from the title song) "wounded in the line of duty.

FIELD COMMANDER COHEN

This song has a more complicated and interesting arrangement than the studio version on *New Skin For The Old Ceremony* five years earlier.

It also includes a stanza ("Drinkin' rum and Coca-Cola / Go down Point Koomahnah / Both mother and daughter / Working for the Yankee dollar") taken from the calypso 'Rum And Coca-Cola', which had been a hit for the Andrews Sisters in 1945. That hit had been copyrighted in the United States by Morey Amsterdam, and Cohen credits the words to him and the music to Jeri Kelli Sullivan and Paul Girlando in the sleeve notes. However, the song was actually written somewhat earlier (and with a rather more caustic social commentary than the more anodyne Andrews Sisters version) by the Trinidadian singer Lord Invader and the composer Lionel Belasco. (Lord Invader and Belasco did later win substantial damages for copyright infringement, but Morey Amsterdam retained the copyright to the song, so Cohen can be acquitted of any involvement in ripping off the original writers.)

THE WINDOW

The first of Cohen's "new" songs on the album, the arrangement is substantially the same as the studio version. Raffi Hakopian contributes a moving violin solo to this rare outing for one of Cohen's most beautiful songs.

THE SMOKEY LIFE

The second "new" song is given a slightly slower and more sultry treatment live, and features Jennifer Warnes duetting with Cohen in a very effective rendition of the song.

THE GYPSY'S WIFE

Completing a trio of "new" songs, 'The Gypsy's Wife' is played in an essentially similar style to the studio version. A particular feature of the live version is the work of Raffi Hakopian on violin and Roscoe Beck on fretless bass.

LOVER LOVER LOVER

The musical backing here is somewhat choppier, and perhaps a little faster, than the original on *New Skin For The Old Ceremony*. It opens with some fine oud playing by John Bilezikjian, who also contributes a solo during the middle section of the song.

HEY, THAT'S NO WAY TO SAY GOODBYE

Cohen revisits his earlier incarnation as a singer-songwriter, but here of course the song is scored for a full band. This amplifies the musical backing, but does not alter the essential tenor of the song. Raffi Hakopian's violin again features.

THE STRANGER SONG

Staying in his singer-songwriter era, Cohen offers a slightly pacier version of 'The Stranger Song', scored for the whole band but with its distinctive guitar figure at the forefront of the arrangement.

Aside from one or two minor changes to the lyrics, there is one significant addition when instead of repeating the line "he wants to trade the game he plays for shelter", Cohen sings "he wants to trade the song he sings for shelter". This underlines the personal nature of the song, despite its use of the third person, and more clearly than in the original version identifies Cohen as the song's protagonist.

THE GUESTS

The fourth and final representative of Cohen's then most recent album, 'The Guests' is again a pretty faithful performance of the studio version, and again enhanced by the violin of Raffi Hakopian and the singing of Sharon Robinson and Jennifer Warnes.

MEMORIES

Perhaps we can hear in this rare live performance of a song from the troubled *Death Of A Ladies' Man* sessions how Cohen really wanted it to sound. Passenger - whose members Cohen name-checks at the end of the song - provide a fifties-style backing to authenticate the High School Prom location of the song (though, as one would expect from Cohen, it is a more direct, carnal and poetic song than is likely to have featured contemporaneously at such an event).

WHY DON'T YOU TRY

The "plinking banjo" of the original has gone, but the band reproduce the rather four-square backing of the original, sounding at times almost like a lounge band. Sharon Robinson duets with Cohen, and Paul Ostermayer decorates it with a sax solo.

Whereas the other songs on *Field Commander Cohen* are presented discretely, 'Why Don't You Try' segues into the following ...

BIRD ON THE WIRE

Apart from the original on *Songs From A Room*, Cohen has released live versions of 'Bird On The Wire' many times - on *Live Songs, Live In Concert, Live In London* and *Songs From The Road* as well as here. This is one of the richest versions, powerfully sung, with interesting changes of tempo, and well decorated by Mitch Watkins' guitar solo.

As usual with his performances of 'Bird On The Wire', there is a notable alteration to the lyrics - the "knight from some old-fashioned book" is here replaced by "a monk bending over the book".

SO LONG, MARIANNE

Backed by the whole band, the arrangement is traditional but necessarily offers a fuller range of musical features than when the song was accompanied by a solo guitar. Cohen gives a powerful and passionate performance that stands up well against the other versions he has recorded.

LIVE IN LONDON

(First issued March 2009)

Cohen began a World Tour on 11 May 2008 in Fredericton, New Brunswick. It ended, after several legs and 246 concerts on 11 December 2010 in The Colosseum at Caesar's Palace, Las Vegas. *Live In London* is the concert performed on 17 July 2008 at the O2 Arena (the former Millennium Dome) in, as the title suggests, London.

The musicians on the tour included several long-time Cohen associates, notably Sharon Robinson (vocals), Bob Metzger (lead and pedal steel guitar) and Roscoe Beck (electric and stand-up bass) who also acted as the tour's musical director. The other members of the band were Rafael Bernardo Gayol (drums and percussion), Neil Larsen (keyboards), Javier Mas (banduria, laud, archilaud and 12-string guitar) and Dino Soldo ("the master of breath on the instruments of wind"). The "sublime Webb Sisters" - Charley and Hattie - provided backing vocals.

The set-list ranged from 'Suzanne' - the first song on Cohen's first album - to 'In My Secret Life' and 'Boogie Street' from *Ten New Songs*. Generally speaking, the arrangements are faithful to the originals, but varnished by the superb and sympathetic musicianship that his fellow performers provided. In terms of performed songs, *Live In London* and the tour it documents must rank as one of Cohen's greatest artistic achievements.

DANCE ME TO THE END OF LOVE

"Thank you so much friends, it's so very kind of you to come to this" Cohen begins. His flattering gratitude to his audience is a recurring theme of his stage announcements during the concert, demonstrating an humility that was doubtless genuine but is nonetheless effective showmanship.

The song is beautifully performed, in substantially the same arrangement as the original version on 'Various Positions'. Javier Mas's delicate embellishments are a particular delight.

THE FUTURE

"It's wonderful to be gathered here on just the other side of intimacy." Who says Cohen has no sense of humour? "I know that some of you have undergone financial and geographical inconvenience [to be here]", besides exhibiting Cohen's elegant and effective use of language, shows an acute understanding of the interrelationship between performer and audience; it is no surprise that this observation is loudly cheered.

Again, this version is insignificantly different from the original on the eponymous album. This time, Bob Metzger's lead guitar provides the notable embellishments.

AIN'T NO CURE FOR LOVE

Cohen opens the song with a witty slice of autobiography, referring to himself at the age of 60 as "just a kid with a crazy dream" (a neat subversion of an old cliché) and listing the drugs he has taken for depression. He has "studied deeply in the philosophies and the religions, but cheerfulness kept breaking through." This appears to accurately reflect the lifting, late in his life, of the clinical depression he had long, if intermittently, suffered from.

Keyboard and, in particular, sax provide the principal decoration in an otherwise unchanged arrangement.

BIRD ON THE WIRE

As has been noted, Cohen has made various changes to the lyrics of 'Bird On The Wire' when performing it live over the years. This version reverts substantially to that sung on *Live Songs*, though the knight is now "bent down " in the old-fashioned book and the woman in her darkened door now only asks for "just a little bit more". (There is also nearly an accidental emendation when Cohen sings "I thought a liar, a lover had to be some kind of liar too", but his hasty correction - with just a hint of a guilty smile in his throat - is Homer nodding not editing.)

Bob Metzger (guitar) and Dino Soldo (sax) play short solos in the middle of the song, and are name-checked having done so.

EVERYBODY KNOWS

Cohen begins this song with speaking the "Old Black Joe" quatrain - perhaps underlining the weight it bears as a bleak social description - before the song proper begins with the conventional words and continues with the standard lyrics and arrangement. Bob Metzger is named for his pedal steel guitar work.

"I wrote that song a long time ago with Sharon Robinson. More recently we wrote ..."

IN MY SECRET LIFE

The original version of 'In My Secret Life' - like all the *Ten New Songs* - was accompanied by electronically-generated music. It is therefore an interesting contrast to hear the song played by live musicians. Apart from the embellishments that are integral to the live performance, and present on the other songs on this album, there is undoubtedly a warmth to the performance to which the live musicians contribute significantly. This is not to disparage the original version, whose sparer arrangement is equally if otherwise engaging. It is consistent in style and tone with its nine companion "new songs", and reflects the deliberate artistic choices of the project. Nonetheless, the comparison of the two versions is an instructive case-study.

As on the original, Sharon Robinson plays a prominent vocal role in this version and is name-checked for her pains, along with the "sublime" Webb Sisters.

WHO BY FIRE

'Who By Fire' opens with long, exquisite archilaud solo by Javier Mas, which appropriately frames this delicate song. Mas plays a shorter solo in the middle of the song, which plays out with a Hammond organ solo by Neil Larsen and a bass solo by Roscoe Beck. (I am not aware of any other instance of a song ending with a bass solo. If it is as unique as my experience suggests, then it is a marvellous bit of musical originality dropped casually into the set.)

The live version of this song does not, of course, resolve an intriguing lyrical ambiguity. Is it "by brave assent" or "by brave ascent"? I personally favour the former reading, as a more plausible counterpoint to the phrase "by accident" which follows it, and because the mountaineering image has already been used in the earlier "by avalanche". But, as always, ambiguity is king.

HEY, THAT'S NO WAY TO SAY GOODBYE

One of Cohen's oldest songs, 'Hey, That's No Way ...' sounds anything but archaic in this lovely version, which showcases Dino Soldo "on the mouth harp" and generally has a much richer musical backing than the more sparsely arranged original. New life is breathed into an old masterpiece.

"Thank you much for your warm hospitality" Cohen tells the audience at the end of the song; "we are so privileged to play for you". Again, Cohen's flattering gratitude subverts the more customary performer-audience relationship. It is of course a conceit that this highly organised, extensive and indeed expensive tour is somehow akin to being invited to perform in someone's house, but it is a conceit that stokes up the feel-good factor and, though it clearly part of the performance, feels nonetheless genuine.

ANTHEM

"Thank you so much friends" he continues. "We are so privileged to be able to gather in moments like these when so much of the world is plunged in darkness and chaos, so ring the bells that still can ring, forget your perfect offering, there is a crack in everything, that's how the light gets in." And the band comes in.

The arrangement is again pretty faithful to the original album version, though Cohen's voice seems gruffer than usual. The song ends with an extended musical coda, Javier Mas to the fore, as the evening's first set come to a close.

 INTRODUCTION

Unlike the other excerpts from Cohen's stage patter, this example - an anecdote about drinking with his "old teacher" Roshi ("excuse me for not dying"), thanking the audience for their support for his career ("for keeping my songs alive") and counselling them not to be alarmed by his computerised keyboard - is specifically identified in the track listing, though it need not be catalogued as one of Cohen's major works.

 TOWER OF SONG

Taken at a slightly slower tempo than the original, this is nonetheless a fine execution of a classic track. The audience cheers wildly when Cohen sings that he was "born with the gift of a golden voice".

The song ends with an extended repetition of the backing vocals ("don't stop, don't leave me here alone" Cohen begs) over which he announces that "tonight ... the great mysteries have unravelled" and that he has "penetrated to the very core of things [and] stumbled on the answer". He cajoles the audience into demanding to be told the philosophical key to the universe, and obliges them by revealing that it is "doo dum dum dum de doo dum dum". His reputation as stand-up comic rises in direct ratio to the ruin of his reputation as a philosopher.

 SUZANNE

It is instructive to compare this version of the first song on Cohen's first album with the original. The song is essentially the same - the lyrics obviously and the signature guitar melody - but the subtle emendations provided by this band clothe the old model in stylish raiment though, as with all good couturiers, one's attention is drawn to the wearer not the worn.

 THE GYPSY'S WIFE

A rare outing for a "middle period" Cohen song, 'The Gypsy's Wife' is taken at a meditative pace, with strong support from the backing vocalists and solos by Javier Mas on banduria at the beginning and Dino Soldo on clarinet in the middle.

Here endeth the first disc.

 BOOGIE STREET

As with 'Suzanne', this live version makes an interesting contrast with the original in terms of how the live band adds texture to it. And the contrast is perhaps richer in that while the original 'Suzanne' was written during Cohen's original "guitar and voice" phase, 'Boogie Street' was the product of a much later project, notable both for its collaborative nature and its use of modern technology. Again, the fundamentals of the song are not altered, but the backing has more swing to it, with even a hint of slow-tempo funk.

The sleeve notes report that the song "features" Sharon Robinson. This rather understates the matter, as it is she who sings the song. Cohen merely provides backing vocals, his ego well under control.

 HALLELUJAH

The original version of 'Hallelujah' recorded in 1984 and included on *Various Positions* differed significantly from the version recorded in 1988 and released on *Live In Concert*. This extended version is a hybrid of the two. It begins with the first two verses of the 1984 version and continues with the third verse of the 1988 version (with some changes, though these may be due to the vagaries of performance rather than considered rewriting). Then come the first two verses of the 1988 version. The final verse is similar in both versions; here it is closer to the 1988 version (but specifying London as the destination to which Cohen "didn't come to fool you").

Musically, the organ work of Neil Larsen is prominent throughout the arrangement.

DEMOCRACY

Cohen uses a variation of the way he opened 'Anthem' here, reciting the final verse before the band comes in. Musically, the arrangement reproduces the studio version, Bob Metzger (guitar) and Dino Soldo (mouth-harp) reprising the distinctive figures of the original. Soldo and Rafael Bernardo Gayol are name-checked during the performance.

I'M YOUR MAN

Rather jauntier than the studio version, this performance highlights Dino Soldo on "the instrument of wind". Lyrically there are fewer variations than in the version performed on *Live In Concert*, though the sands across which Cohen offers to walk are now "burning".

That Cohen has the audience in the palm of his hand is evidenced by the cheers that greet his offer to "examine every inch of you" (though the volume of the cheers suggests that maybe one half of his audience is keener on the examination than the other half).

RECITATION

Although accompanied by Neil Larsen's keyboards, this is a poem not a song. It appears to bear no resemblance to 'A Thousand Kisses Deep' on *Ten New Songs*. However, in Cohen's 2006 anthology *Book of Longing*, the text appears as Part 1 of a poem called 'Thousand Kisses Deep'. Part 2 consists of the lyrics of the song.

TAKE THIS WALTZ

The arrangement accentuates a somewhat plodding waltz rhythm. That this is deliberate rather than the work of second-rate musicians is proven by the beautiful little decorations that the band variously contribute and by the feeling of slightly threadbare jollity they achieve, which perfectly underscores the melancholy lyrics.

At the end of the song, Cohen introduces the band, with florid poeticism. Javier Mas is "the sweet shepherd of strings", Dino Soldo "the master of breath", Bob Metzger "the signature of steady", Rafael Bernardo Gayol "the prince of precision", though Neil Larsen is merely "impeccable". "My collaborator" Sharon Robinson is "incomparable" and the Webb Sisters once again "sublime". Musical Director and bassist Roscoe Beck is "our guardian and sentry". Finally, Cohen thanks "my friends" the audience. "Thank you for a memorable evening" he says, and if there is of course some conventional politeness in his thanks, listeners to the album will undoubtedly conclude that he speaks no more than the truth.

SO LONG, MARIANNE

Cohen gives a passionate rendition of this old song, underlining the depths of (undoubtedly personal) emotion that it embraces and which was perhaps underplayed in the more stoical and musically simpler original version.

The arrangement mirrors the original in being strongly guitar-based - another interesting example of how Cohen's band can both reproduce and embellish his material - with a notable contribution by Dino Soldo on the mouth-harp (that ubiquitous accompaniment to the sixties singer-songwriter).

FIRST WE TAKE MANHATTAN
From reproducing a sixties guitar and voice style, the band shows its versatility by changing gear for the much rockier feel of this song from *The Future*. Roscoe Beck's bass thunders through the opening chords, and there is driving organ work from Neil Larsen. Rafael Bernardo Gayol's drums are more prominent, and certainly thumped harder, than on many songs in the set. Yet there is subtlety too - Javier Mas's delicate picking seems, at the appropriate moment, to imitate a "plywood violin".

Vocal duties are shared with Sharon Robinson and the Webbs in what is an excellent ensemble piece.

 SISTERS OF MERCY
Then the mood changes again and we are treated to a superb version of one of Cohen's earliest songs. It is taken at a slow tempo, slower even than the original, but this showcases the band's artistry - as with riding a bicycle, it requires more skill and balance to go slowly (at least without wobbling all over the place) than to go faster. And Javier Mas contributes an exquisite archilaud solo.

The final, repeated lines - "we weren't lovers like that and besides it would still be all right" - remind us what a generous song 'Sisters of Mercy' is and what a compassionate writer Cohen can be.

 IF IT BE YOUR WILL
"It was a while ago, faced with some obstacles, that I wrote this song, well it's more of a prayer." Cohen goes on to recite the first verse and a half, before handing over to the Webb Sisters, who sing a beautiful and powerful version, augmented by Hattie Webb's harp playing.

Cohen has described 'If It Be Your Will' as "probably one of the best songs I've ever written". Even if critics may rate several other of his songs higher in their pantheon, it is clearly a song that means a lot to its author,

so it is generous indeed of him to stand aside and let others sing it at his concert. But it is not mere altruism that motivates him but also the artistic integrity of the piece. It is a delicate song, and it gains greatly from the higher register (and, it must be said, more technically accomplished) voices of Charley and Hattie Webb.

 CLOSING TIME
And from the sublimity of the Webb Sisters, the concert changes tack again, into the netherworld of the public house and the rousing hoe-down of 'Closing Time'. Faithful though it is in its arrangement, this version perhaps loses some of the dark seriousness of the original. But maybe we don't need a heavy final course to this extended banquet, and an up-tempo ending is an appropriate way to send the audience on their journey home.

"Closing time friends, thank so much" Cohen ends ...

 I TRIED TO LEAVE YOU
... but it would be too corny to close with 'Closing Time' wouldn't it? And wouldn't a song about being unable to leave not be a fitting follow-up?

This lengthy version, the second longest song on the album, showcases the whole band, with solos successively from Bob Metzger (electric guitar), Dino Soldo (saxophone), Neil Larsen (Hammond E3), Sharon Robinson (vocals), Javier Mas (archilaud), the Webb Sisters (vocals, largely non-verbal humming), Roscoe Beck (bass) and Rafael Bernardo Gayol (drums). There are loud cheers when Cohen, singing the concluding verse, reaches the words "I hope you're satisfied" and "a man still working".

 WHITHER THOU GOEST
Finally, Cohen sends the audience gently into the good night with this short valediction, a 1954 song by Guy Singer based on words from the biblical Book of Ruth. After the banquet, a sorbet to end with.

LIVE AT THE ISLE OF WIGHT 1970

(First issued October 2009)

Cohen began his set at the third Isle of Wight Festival in the small hours of 31 August 1970. The Festival had ambitions to be an English Woodstock - Jimi Hendrix was the headline act in a stellar line-up - and it mimicked the original Woodstock insofar as many more people than expected turned up, eventually forcing the organisers to declare it a free festival. Despite this generosity, the mood of the crowd was ugly - bottles had been thrown at Kris Kristofferson and he had been booed off stage - though tiredness had taken the edge off the aggression by the time, well behind schedule, that Cohen took the stage.

Cohen performed with The Army, with whom he was currently touring Europe and with whom he had been working in the studio on the sessions that eventually produced *Songs Of Love And Hate*. The Army consisted of Bob Johnston (Cohen's producer on *Songs From A Room*, then riding high in the British charts), Ron Cornelius, Charlie Daniels and Bubba Fowler, with Corlynn Hanney, Susan Musmanno and Donna Washburn providing backing vocals. As well as the songs described below, Cohen included poems in the set, and introduced it with a request to the audience to light matches (arguably an unwise suggestion given that one of the reasons his appearance had been delayed was that the stage had earlier been set on fire) thus, perhaps unwittingly starting a trend that later became a ubiquitous feature of MOR concerts.

The quality of recording equipment available today, and regularly used even at the most minor of gigs, was not around in 1970, so the recording is not technically perfect. As Steve Berkowitz (Executive Producer of the DVD than accompanies the album) put it in his sleeve notes: "Buzzes, microphone dropouts, clunks, feedback are all part of the set and performance ... efforts to remove them would be futile and the results less true". And it may be fairly said that anyone whose enjoyment of the album is spoiled by its technical imperfections has rather missed the point.

BIRD ON THE WIRE

A slowish reading of this classic song (at one point a voice - presumably one of the band - says "let's pick it up a bit"), this version offers the earliest recorded outing of the emendation "I thought a lover had to be some kind of liar too" discussed in *Live Songs* above. There is an additional emendation - "I have saved all my sorrows for you" - which has not survived into subsequent performances of this much-edited song.

SO LONG, MARIANNE

Cohen's poignant and perhaps slightly desperate introduction ("I wrote this for Marianne, I hope she's here, maybe she's here, I hope she's here") precedes a heartfelt performance of the classic arrangement of the song. As with many songs on the album, Cohen is accompanied by the band but his acoustic guitar is a predominant feature.

YOU KNOW WHO I AM

Taken at a slightly slower tempo than on *Songs From A Room*, 'You Know Who I Am' is given a delicate treatment that neither adds to nor subtracts from the recorded version.

LADY MIDNIGHT

Another song that faithfully reproduces its classic arrangement. Towards the end, Cohen tries to engender some audience participation ("won't you surrender with me?" he asks), but the hour was late and the crowd shows no eagerness to join in the performance.

ONE OF US CANNOT BE WRONG

Cohen introduces 'One Of Us Cannot Be Wrong' with a description of its genesis. It was apparently written in "a peeling room in the Chelsea Hotel" - "before I was rich and famous and they gave me well-painted rooms" he goes on boast - when he was "coming off amphetamine and pursuing a blonde lady that I met in a Nazi poster". The "thin green candle" that the singer lights was one of the rituals Cohen performed to win her, though he does not specifically advise us that it was a successful technique.

Again, 'One Of Us Cannot Be Wrong' differs little in its arrangement from the studio version, though it well performed with a haunting flute coda. There is a minor addition to the lyrics. After the reference to "the dress that you wore for the world to look through" Cohen adds the observation "and the world looked through", betraying perhaps some of the personal bitterness that he had alchemised into the song.

THE STRANGER SONG

Cohen's voice seems to have mellowed as the night wore on, having sometimes sounded a little hoarse earlier in the set (and indeed sometimes later on too), and is in fine form in this lovely performance of the song in its classic arrangement.

TONIGHT WILL BE FINE

This performance was included on Cohen's first live album *Live Songs*.

HEY, THAT'S NO WAY TO SAY GOODBYE

By way of introduction, Cohen buffs up his counter-cultural credentials, though perhaps more as Cassandra than Messiah, by announcing that "they've surrounded the island: one of these days we're going to have the land for our own, we're not strong enough yet, you can't fool yourselves". He then delivers a fine version of one of his greatest love songs.

DIAMONDS IN THE MINE

The first of three as yet unreleased songs that were to appear the following year on *Songs Of Love And Hate*, 'Diamonds In The Mine' is introduced with a verse (that isn't in the studio version) in which Cohen offers an interesting assessment of his songwriting. "They gave me some money for my sad and famous song / They said 'the crowd is waiting; hurry up or they'll be gone / But I could not change my style and I guess I never will / So I sing this for the poison snakes on Devastation Hill". Of course, 'Diamonds In The Mine' is itself something of a change of style, and his prediction of the immutability of his style would not be borne out by his later work.

The arrangement is generally the same as that later released, although the backing singers use a subtly different melody when repeating "there are no diamonds in the mine". The lyrics show two differences from the studio version. The first - singing the second couplet of the second stanza as the second couplet of the first stanza - may be a simple mistake on the night, as he repeats it when he gets to the second stanza. The second - following "there is no comfort in the covens of the witch" with the line "there's no easy way to tell you who is poor and who is rich" - is probably an earlier version amended when the album version was recorded.

SUZANNE

From a new song, Cohen turns to one of his oldest and gives a classic performance of a classic song in its classic arrangement.

SING ANOTHER SONG, BOYS

At the last minute, this version replaced the studio version on *Songs Of Love And Hate* the following year.

THE PARTISAN

Cohen dedicated this performance of 'The Partisan' to Joan Baez (who had performed earlier that evening) and to "the work she is doing", a rare Cohen nod to active political engagement. The version sung here follows the original arrangement on *Songs From A Room*.

FAMOUS BLUE RAINCOAT

Cohen introduces 'Famous Blue Raincoat' ("not that I want to be coy") as "maybe ... good music to make love to". Fine song though it is, one might plausibly dispute his judgement. I would wager it would come low in any poll of the public's favourite romance-enhancing songs.

'Famous Blue Raincoat' had not been released at this point, though it would soon be included on *Songs Of Love And Hate*. The version played here is substantially the same as the later studio version, though there is a rather fetching guitar figure that does not make it onto the later version.

SEEMS SO LONG AGO, NANCY

Introduced with almost Cleudo-like precision ("in the bathroom" with "her brother's shotgun"), this version replicates both musically and lyrically the version included on *Songs From A Room*. Though a well-realised version of the song, it is noteworthy that only fifteen months later Cohen recorded a subtly revised version that was included on (and is discussed under) *Live Songs*.

SONGS FROM THE ROAD

(First issued September 2010)

Songs From The Road is a collection of performances from various concerts in 2008 and 2009 on Cohen's World Tour, selected by producer Ed Sanders as "special moments" based partly on his contemporaneous notes and observations and partly on after-show conversations with Cohen as they drove back to the hotel. Sanders reports that these after-show conversations were usually restricted to "silence or trivialities" but that special performances ("when a song had found that 'secret chord'") would elicit Cohen's retrospective commentary.

Songs From The Road is a companion piece to *Live In London*, taken as it is from the same tour and, therefore, with the same musicians. Whereas *Live In London* presents a single concert, here twelve different evenings are represented (though the album is mixed seamlessly so that one could hear it and imagine that the songs were performed sequentially on the same night). Four of the songs on *Songs From The Road* also appear on *Live In London*, which allows a fascinating comparison between different performances of the same arrangements by the same musicians. Of the other eight songs, some were regularly played during the Tour, while 'Avalanche' had a mere seven outings in October 2008.

As well as being a valuable addition to the archive of Cohen's World Tour, *Songs From The Road* - doubtless because it is made up of memorable performances - seems collectively to enhance the significance of the songs it contains, and to increase their relative importance in the not insubstantial canon of Cohen's great songs.

LOVER LOVER LOVER
Fittingly for a song written in the Sinai desert, 'Lover Lover Lover' was recorded at the Ramat Gan Stadium in Tel Aviv, on the last night of Summer 2009 leg of the Tour.

Ed Sanders reports "50,000 green glow-sticks lighting up one magical night" and one can almost sense the Israeli autumn as "the spirit of this song … rise(s) up pure and free".

BIRD ON THE WIRE
The first of the songs that has also appeared on *Live In London*, this version is necessarily similar, with Bob Metzger and Dino Sold soloing at the same point. The fascination is in the minor differences in their solos. Here, both are magically fluent and produce what Ed Sanders describes as "two of their best".

Recorded on 6 November 2008 at the Clyde Auditorium, Glasgow, Cohen again alters the lyrics of his most revised song. He drops the "beggar/pretty woman" quatrain, replacing it with a stanza similar to that used in the *Live In Concert* version: "I say don't cry … any more / It's over now, it's done, it has been paid for / I say don't cry … you were always the one / It was you that this longing was made for". My personal view is that this emendation works less well than the original next but, hey, it's not my song.

CHELSEA HOTEL
Somewhat to the surprise of the band, Cohen had given a solo rendition of 'Chelsea Hotel' one night in Rotterdam. Having rehearsed it with the band, he incorporated it into the set. This performance, recorded at the Royal Albert

Hall, London, was the second outing for the full band version.

Sung - and superbly - by a much older man than the one who wrote, the song's elegaic tone is enhanced by the lifetime of experience that now inhabits Cohen's voice, underlined by the slower tempo this version is taken at. That the song was originally written in the past tense, as a piece of reportage, means that it works well, if not better, with the passage of time.

Cohen makes one small lyrical adjustment in this version. Whereas she had originally "just turned your back on the crowd", now she "just threw it all to the ground", a detail that improves the song by hinting at a wilful recklessness rather than simply a Garboesque asociality.

HEART WITH NO COMPANION
This first class performance at the Oberhausen King Pilsener Arena in Germany on 2 November 2008 reportedly produced the greatest and most sustained applause of the entire tour. ('Hallelujah' normally topped the clapometer ratings.)

Taken at the same jaunty pace as the original, this version features fine work from Bob Metzger (pedal steel guitar), Dino Soldo (harmonica) and Neil Larsen (piano).

THAT DON'T MAKE IT JUNK
An excellent rendition, with a splendid contribution from Dino Soldo's harmonica, this was recorded at the O2 Arena London on 13 November 2008 (some four months after the concert captured on *Live In London* at the same venue).

WAITING FOR THE MIRACLE
Exactly a year later, 'Waiting For The Miracle' was recorded at the HP Pavilion, San José, California. This concert was the last one of 2009 and if Cohen and his colleagues were weary after a year and a half on the road, this fine performance demonstrates that they were also "match fit" after an extensive run of concerts.

AVALANCHE

'Avalanche' was played for the first time on the tour on 4 October 2008 and for the last time 19 days later after a mere seven performances. This version was recorded midway through the song's "run", on 12 October in Sweden's Gothenburg Scandinavium. It has a fittingly sparse arrangement, featuring Cohen's own guitar work (and in fine form he is too).

SUZANNE

The second song that had already appeared on *Live In London*, this version was recorded on 30 November 2008, the last date of that leg of the tour, at the MENA Arena, Manchester. Unlike 'Bird On The Wire', 'Suzanne' has remained unchanged throughout Cohen's career and this version is very similar to the *Live In London* one. 'Suzanne' was played on every night of the tour and Ed Sanders believes this version possesses "a special timeless beauty all of its own". This is undoubtedly a fine version. Fans could spend hours debating the merits of the two versions, but a phrase involving "angels" and "pin-heads" springs to mind - a better course would be simply to enjoy whichever version one is listening to at any given time.

THE PARTISAN

Ed Sanders reports in the sleevenotes that, after a few days off, band members often became anxious to perform and played particularly well when they next took the stage. This apparently happened with Javier Mas in Helsinki on 10 October 2008 at the Hartwall Arena.

Sanders also says that Cohen looked "every part the underground freedom fighter with his slightly scruffy, unshaven appearance". Be that as it may (and the photos of Cohen on this tour more usually show him in dapper mode), the deeper voice of his later career adds a distinct and effective resonance to the performance, and age gives greater authenticity to the tiredness and privation that the song portrays. All in all, a fine performance.

FAMOUS BLUE RAINCOAT

This version of 'Famous Blue Raincoat' was recorded at the same concert as 'That Don't Make It Junk'. Ed Sanders, who had not wanted to include two songs from the same concert on this album, states that he saw the song "performed many times but this is the magical one". Indeed it is, with Cohen in fine voice and Dino Soldo starring on "the instrument of wind".

HALLELUJAH

The third song that was also on *Live In London*, this version was recorded at the Coachella Music Festival in Indio, California on 17 April 2009. The lyrics mirror the London version, with the same verses sung in the same order, though this time Cohen avers that he "didn't come to Coachella just to fool you". (It is an amusing paradox that Cohen invariably uses the song with the most ancient setting to name-check his current location.)

CLOSING TIME

The fourth song to appear on both albums from the 2008/10 tour, this version was recorded on 24 May 2009 at the John Labatt Centre, London, Ontario. Ed Sanders reports how much Cohen enjoyed playing in his native land, and how much his audiences appreciated him there, and there is certainly a sense of enjoyment permeating this version of 'Closing Time', witness some of the musical flourishes towards the end. There are certainly diamonds in this mine.

PART III
COMPILATION
ALBUMS

GREATEST HITS/THE BEST OF LEONARD COHEN

(First issued November 1975)

After four studio albums and one live one, it was decided to release a compilation. Cohen has said he was "against the idea at first, but I don't remember why I was convinced of it". His biographer Ira B. Nadel claims Cohen agreed "because there was a new generation of listeners and because he was given complete artistic control". Cohen certainly exercised artistic control, not only picking the songs himself but also writing his own sleevenotes and designing the package. It was at his insistence that the lyrics of all the songs were included.

The album contains four songs from *Songs Of Leonard Cohen*, three from *Songs From A Room*, two from *Songs Of Love And Hate*, and three from *New Skin For The Old Ceremony*. No songs were selected from *Live Songs*, and no live or alternate versions were chosen. Obviously every Cohen aficionado will lament the absence of a particular favourite. (I would argue that 'Seems So Long Ago, Nancy' and 'Tonight Will Be Fine' had earned their right to be there, but that is by-the-by and of course it is a selection not a collection.) Nonetheless, the twelve songs offer a balanced retrospective of his career up to that point. However, the selection does tend to stress the "singer with guitar" side of Cohen's work, at the expense of the fuller, rockier style that had marked some of the songs on *Songs Of Love And Hate* (e.g.

'Diamonds In the Mine') or *New Skin For The Old Ceremony* (e.g. 'Is This What You Wanted'). Similarly, Cohen's burgeoning stage skills went unrepresented.

The album was titled *The Best Of Leonard Cohen* in North America and Japan, while in the rest of the world it was called simply *Greatest Hits*. It was a hit in Europe, Cohen's major market during the Seventies. In the USA, it did not trouble the charts.

All tracks have been discussed elsewhere. The track listing is as follows: 'Suzanne', 'Sisters Of Mercy', 'So Long, Marianne', 'Bird On The Wire', 'Lady Midnight', 'The Partisan', 'Hey, That's No Way To Say Goodbye', 'Famous Blue Raincoat', 'Last Year's Man', 'Chelsea Hotel #2', 'Who By Fire', 'Take This Longing'.

The album was re-released in July 2009 with updated artwork and a revised track listing to take account of Cohen's work since 1975. The new track listing is: 'Suzanne', 'So Long, Marianne', 'Sisters Of Mercy', 'Famous Blue Raincoat', 'Everybody Knows', 'Waiting For The Miracle', 'Who By Fire', 'Chelsea Hotel number 2', 'Hey, That's No Way To Say Goodbye', 'Bird On The Wire', 'A Thousand Kisses Deep', 'The Future', 'Closing Time', 'Dance Me To The End Of Love', 'First We Take Manhattan', 'I'm Your Man', 'Hallelujah'.

MORE BEST OF LEONARD COHEN

(First issued 1997)

"I never felt there was any great urgency for another compilation album, but it was the 30th anniversary of my connection with [Columbia/CBS] and although I myself feel very little nostalgia, I went along with it. I did choose the songs." In doing so, Cohen selected only from his two previous studio albums (four songs each from *I'm Your Man* and *The Future*) and his most recent live album (three songs were selected), adding two previously unreleased songs as a bonus.

The album represents a very fair sampler of Cohen's work over the last decade, and it is hard to argue that it does not contain all his "greatest hits" from this period. It is interesting to note that, taking his two compilation albums together, Cohen has directly anthologised nothing from *Death Of A Ladies' Man*, *Recent Songs* or *Various Positions* (though both 'Dance Me To The End Of Love' and 'Hallelujah', included live on this album, first appeared on the latter).

The following tracks have already been discussed elsewhere: 'Everybody Knows', 'I'm Your Man', 'Take This Waltz', 'Tower Of Song', 'Anthem', 'Democracy', 'The Future', 'Closing Time', 'Dance Me To The End Of Love', 'Suzanne', 'Hallelujah'

NEVER ANY GOOD

While it would be wrong to call this a great, lost Cohen masterpiece, it is a pleasant enough bonus. Backed by bar-band-style good rocking with a solid horn section swinging along behind it, 'Never Any Good' is a entertaining excursion to a familiar corner of the Cohen theme park where the failed lover growls an insouciant, and slightly defiant, apology. With all the confidence of a man who, having learnt from his mistakes, can repeat them with precision, Cohen applies his literary and musical skills to seducing his beloved into leaving him.

There are some fine Cohen touches. "I bet my life on you / But you called me and I folded" is not only a coherent metaphor taken from the card-table, but contains the ambiguity that "called" could mean "rang" and "folded" could mean "crumpled", which puts a different complexion on the sentence. His description of the female body ("those holy hills, that deep ravine") is sensual without being smutty, and also utilises an old Cohen trick – the use of a religious adjective in a secular context. And the phrase "I'm sorry for my crimes against the moonlight" would not have been out of place on any Cohen album of the last thirty years.

THE GREAT EVENT

How typical of Cohen that, for the last track of his then latest album, he should choose to experiment! The song, if song it be, consists of a scale-like keyboard phrase backing the recitation of a poem welcoming the forthcoming end of the world, to be triggered by the artist playing the 'Moonlight Sonata' backwards at dusk next Tuesday. The recitation is credited to "Victoria", for whom English is obviously not a first language, if indeed it is a language she speaks at all. Her stresses are all wrong, her emphases those of someone reading a foreign text. That this is a deliberately sought effect, underlining the "strangeness" of the poet's words, is clear from the muddy distortion of the vocal track. Cohen appears only briefly, double-tracking the phrase "what a sigh of relief" towards the end of the piece.

A wise man once said that no experiment is a failure. While it would be hard to claim that 'The Great Event' is a triumphant success, one can heave one's own "sigh of relief" that Cohen is still able to experiment towards the end of his career. Indeed, there is something of the wheel turning full circle about this track, for one can easily imagine just such a piece emerging from the Montreal avant-garde of the Fifties in which Cohen first cut his artistic teeth.

THE ESSENTIAL LEONARD COHEN

(First issued 2002)

This collection was released as part of Sony's *The Essential* series, and covers all Cohen's studio albums up to 2002 with the exception of *Death Of A Ladies' Man*. All tracks were digitally remastered by Cohen and Bob Ludwig. A third disc was added when the collection was re-issued in 2008 as part of *The Essential 3.0* series.

Disc 1 contains: 'Suzanne', 'The Stranger Song', 'Sisters Of Mercy', 'Hey, That's No Way To Say Goodbye', 'So Long, Marianne', 'Bird On The Wire', 'The Partisan', 'Famous Blue Raincoat', 'Chelsea Hotel number 2', 'Take This Longing', 'Who By Fire', 'The Guests', 'Hallelujah', 'If It Be Your Will', 'Night Comes On', 'I'm Your Man', 'Everybody Knows' and 'Tower Of Song'.

Disc 2 contains: 'Ain't No Cure For Love', 'Take This Waltz', 'First We Take Manhattan', 'Dance Me To The End Of Love', The Future', 'Democracy', 'Waiting For The Miracle', 'Closing Time', 'Anthem', In My Secret Life', 'Alexandra Leaving', 'A Thousand Kisses Deep' and 'Love Itself'.

Disc 3 (billed as a selection of fans' favourites) contains: 'Seems So Long Ago, Nancy', Love Calls You By Your Name', ' A Singer Must Die', 'Death Of A Ladies' Man', 'The Traitor', 'By The Rivers Dark' and 'The Letters'.

THE COMPLETE STUDIO ALBUMS COLLECTION

(First issued 2011)

The Complete Studio Albums Collection contains all 11 of Leonard Cohen's remastered studio albums packaged in a special box along with a lavish 36-page booklet including all discographical annotations and recording information, as well as a 1,300-word essay by Pico Iyer.

Disc 1: *Songs Of Leonard Cohen*; Disc 2: *Songs From A Room*; Disc 3: *Songs Of Love And Hate* ; Disc 4: *New Skin For The Old Ceremony*; Disc 5: *Death Of A Ladies' Man;* Disc 6: *Recent Songs*; Disc 7: *Various Positions*; Disc 8: *I'm Your Man*; Disc 9: *The Future*; Disc 10: *Ten New Songs*; Disc 11: *Dear Heather*.

THE COMPLETE ALBUMS COLLECTION

(First issued 2011)

The Complete Albums Collection contains all 17 Leonard Cohen albums – both live and remastered studio recordings along with the 36-page booklet including all discographical annotations and recording information, as well as the 1,300-word essay by Pico Iyer.

Disc 1: *Songs Of Leonard Cohen*; Disc 2: *Songs From A Room*; Disc 3: *Songs Of Love And Hate*; Disc 4: *Live Songs*; Disc 5: *New Skin For The Old Ceremony*; Disc 6: *Death Of A Ladies' Man*; Disc 7: *Recent Songs*; Disc 8: *Various Positions*; Disc 9: *I'm Your Man*; Disc 10: *The Future*; Disc 11: *Cohen Live*; Disc 12: *Field Commander Cohen*; Disc 13: *Ten New Songs*; Disc 14: *Dear Heather*; Disc 15: *Live In London* (First CD Of 2-Disc Set); Disc 16: *Live In London* (Second CD Of 2-Disc Set); Disc 17: *Live At The Isle Of Wight 1970*; Disc 18: *Songs From The Road*.

PART IV
MISCELLANEO
RECORDINGS

US

SINGLES

Cohen is not essentially a singles artist. Various tracks in various combinations have been issued as singles, EPs or maxi-singles in various countries. However, all such tracks appear on substantive Cohen albums, with one exception - a 1976 single containing live versions of 'Do I Have To Dance All Night' and 'The Butcher'. The details of Cohen's non-album records will only be of interest to collectors and completists. They will have better sources for the information they seek than I do, so I will say no more on the subject.

OTHER RECORDINGS

Apart from several poetry readings, which are outside the scope of this work, a number of other Cohen recordings have been included on various albums during his career.

'Tonight Will Be Fine', recorded at the 1970 Isle of Wight Festival, was included on the 1971 album *The First Great Rock Festivals Of The Seventies – Isle of Wight / Atlanta*. This is the same version Cohen included on *Live Songs*. A recording of 'Suzanne' from the same gig was included on a 1995 compilation album celebrating the festival's 25th anniversary.

'Take This Waltz' was included on the 1986 Lorca tribute album *Poetas En Nueva York*. A remixed version of the song was included on *I'm Your Man*.

Live versions of 'I'm Your Man' and 'Coming Back To You' recorded at the Complex in Los Angeles on 18 April 1993 were included on a compilation called *The Columbia Radio Hour* released in 1994.

In addition, Cohen sang lead vocal on the David and Don Was song 'Elvis' Rolls Royce' which appeared on the 1990 Was (Not Was) album *are you okay?* Cohen also duetted with Elton John on his 1993 album *Duets*, singing Ted Daffan's 1943 song 'Born To Lose'.

Although he did not perform on it, Cohen produced and wrote the lyrics for Anjani Thomas's 2006 album *Blue Alert*,

TRIBUTE ALBUMS

Five albums have been released containing covers of Cohen songs performed by various artists.

FAMOUS BLUE RAINCOAT

(First issued 1986)

Jennifer Warnes' album (originally to have been called 'Jenny Sings Lenny') has been credited with re-establishing Cohen's reputation in North America. It contains one song Cohen has not himself recorded, 'Song Of Bernadette', which he wrote with Warnes, she supplying the music for his words. The album was a hit in America and a number one in the UK, and earned a gold disc in Canada.

The track listing is as follows: 'First We Take Manhattan', 'Bird On A Wire' (sic), 'Famous Blue Raincoat', 'Joan Of Arc' (on which Cohen duets with Warnes), 'Ain't No Cure For Love', 'Coming Back To You', 'Song Of Bernadette', 'A Singer Must Die', 'Came So Far For Beauty'

I'M YOUR FAN

(First issued 1991)

The genesis of this album was a chance conversation between The Pixies' Francis Black and Christian Fevret, editor of the French music magazine *Les Inrockuptibles*. The album generated enormous interest in Cohen's work among a section of the public that might not otherwise have been exposed to it. Cohen has acknowledged that he was "very touched" by this "kind of gift". A particular highlight is Nick Cave's radical re-working of 'Tower Of Song' ("I said to Lenny Cohen, 'How lonely does it get?' ").

The track listing is as follows: 'Who By Fire' (performed by The House of Love), 'Hey, That's No Way To Say Goodbye' (Ian McCulloch), 'I Can't Forget' (The Pixies), 'Stories Of The Street' (That Petrol Emotion), 'Bird On The Wire' (The Lilac Time), 'Suzanne' (Geoffrey Oryema), 'So Long, Marianne' (James), 'Avalanche IV' ([in French] by Jean-Louis Murat), 'Don't Go Home With Your Hard-On' (David McComb and Adam Peters), 'First We Take Manhattan' (R.E.M.), 'Chelsea Hotel' (sic) (Lloyd Cole), 'Tower Of Song' (Robert Foster), 'Take This Longing' (Peter Astor), 'True Love Leaves No Traces' (Dead Famous People), 'I'm Your Man' (Bill Pritchard), 'A Singer Must Die' (Fatima Mansions), 'Tower Of Song' (Nick Cave and The Bad Seeds), 'Hallelujah' (John Cale).

TOWER OF SONG

(First issued 1995)

Conceived by Cohen's manager Kelley Lynch as a 60th birthday present (in the event, a belated one), this album was well received both by the birthday boy himself ("I like this album... I can play it in my jeep without fear") and by the general public, especially in Canada where it earned a gold disc.

The track listing is as follows: 'Everybody Knows' performed by Don Henley, 'Coming Back To You' (Trisha Yearwood), 'Sisters Of Mercy' (Sting and The Chieftains), 'Hallelujah' (Bono), 'Famous Blue Raincoat' (Tori Amos), 'Ain't No Cure For Love' (Aaron Neville), 'I'm Your Man' (Elton John), 'Bird On A Wire' (sic) (Willie Nelson), 'Suzanne' (Peter Gabriel), 'Light As The Breeze' (Billy Joel), 'If It Be Your Will' (Jann Arden), 'Story Of Isaac' (Suzanne Vega), 'Coming Back To You' (Martin Gore).

LEONARD COHEN: I'M YOUR MAN

COHEN: THE SCANDINAVIAN REPORT

(First issued 2006)

(First issued 2009)

This is the soundtrack of the eponymous film by Lian Lunson about Cohen's life and career, based on a tribute show performed in January 2005 at the Sydney Opera House, although the performances on the album were mostly recorded at an earlier incarnation of the show performed in Brighton in May 2004. Cohen's performance with U2 was not recorded live but was performed specifically for the film in New York in May 2005.

The track listing is as follows: 'Tower Of Song' performed by Martha Wainwright, 'Tonight Will Be Fine' (Teddy Thompson), 'I'm Your Man' (Nick Cave), 'Winter Lady' (Kate and Anna McGarrigle), 'Sisters Of Mercy' (Beth Orton), 'Chelsea Hotel number 2' (Rufus Wainright), 'If It Be Your Will' (Anthony), 'I Can't Forget' (Jarvis Cocker), 'Famous Blue Raincoat' (The Handsome Family), 'Bird On The Wire' (Perla Batalla), 'Everybody Knows' (Rufus Wainwright), 'The Traitor' (Martha Wainwright), 'Suzanne' (Nick Cave, Perla Batalla and Julie Christensen), 'The Future' (Teddy Thompson), 'Anthem' (Perla Batalla and Julie Christensen), 'Tower Of Song' (Leonard Cohen and U2) plus 'The Guests' (Laurie Anderson), an iTunes Store bonus track.

Conceived by producer Lars Halapi and A&R man Lars "Billy" Hansson, *The Scandinavian Report* was recorded at Studio 4, Radiohuset, Stockholm over two days in August 2009.

The track listing is as follows: 'First We Take Manhattan' performed by Cookies n Beans, 'Here It Is' (Rebecka Törnkvist), 'If It Be Your Will' (Moto Boy), 'Dansa Mig Till Kärlekens Slut [Dance Me To The End of Love]' (Jan Malmsjö), 'Ain't No Cure For Love' (Ane Brun), 'Everybody Knows' (Bo Sundström), 'Hey, That's No Way To Say Goodbye' (Sara Isaksson), 'Sisters Of Mercy' (Lars Halapi), 'USA Är Redo För Demokrati [Democracy]' (Mikael Wiehe), 'Hallelujah' (Anders Widmark), 'Bird On The Wire' (Eva Dahlgren), 'In My Secret Life' (Vidar & Peter), 'The Partisan' (Jenny Wilson), 'Chelsea Hotel number 2' (Olle Ljungström), 'Waiting For The Miracle To Come' (Sophie Zelmani), 'Suzanne' (Christel Alsos).